EAT THE WEEDS

Other Books by Ben Charles Harris

KITCHEN MEDICINES

Barre Publishers 1968

BETTER HEALTH WITH CULINARY HERBS

Privately Printed in 1952

EAT
THE
WEEDS

BEN CHARLES HARRIS

BARRE PUBLISHING
BARRE, MASSACHUSETTS
DISTRIBUTED BY CROWN
PUBLISHERS, INC.
NEW YORK

Fifth Printing, April, 1975

Library of Congress Catalog Card Number 69-12302
Printed in the United States of America

To My Weed-Eating Sons
Irwin, Saul, Herbert and Alan

CONTENTS

And God said, "Behold, I have given you every herb bearing seed, which is upon the face of all the earth, and every tree, in the which is the fruit of a tree yielding seed, to you it shall be for meat.

"And to every beast of the earth, and to every fowl of the air, and to every thing that creepeth upon the earth, wherein there is life, I have given every green herb for meat: and it was so." *Genesis* 1:29, 30.

EAT THE WEEDS

Introduction

In New England, there are some 150 excellent substitutes for store-bought and even garden-cultivated vegetables and fruits. True, they are generally considered by some as "grass" or "weeds," garden nuisances or uninvited guests to one's lawn. These food substitutes abound in Mother Nature's vast produce garden and are to be found in field and forest, gardens, lawns and waste piles, roadsides, swamps and brooks. A few more adventurous souls have at one time or another eaten such commoners as Dandelion and Watercress leaves, Milkweed shoots, Mushrooms, Burdock stems and Blueberries and Crabapples—and are none the worse for it. And, moreover, let us not overlook the fact that right on our own pantry shelves or in our refrigerators are many such store-bought items which we take so much for granted: jellies and preserves of Blueberry and Blackberry, Cranberry sauce, Wild Rice, Mushrooms, Maple Syrup and Iodine Ration Tablets (composed of Kelp, a seaweed).

Such native edibles may well boast of their food values, possessing in many instances far more health-fortifying nutritive, mineral-vitamin principles than many garden vegetables: Watercress contains three times as much Vitamin E as Lettuce and almost three times as much calcium as Spinach. Dandelion offers six times the quantity of Vitamin A and more than twice that of the calcium, phosphorus and iron contained in garden Lettuce. Throughout medical history, friend

Burdock has well earned its reputation as a "blood purifier" and today this property is ascertained by its much
needed blood-fortifying minerals of calcium, silicon and
sulphur.

To fully comprehend the relationship of herbs to
food and a more precise definition of "herb," it is important to define the relationship of herbs to our everyday vegetables. According to one of America's foremost
horticulturalists, Prof. L. H. Bailey, in his *Standard Cyclopedia of Horticulture*, a vegetable "is an edible herbaceous plant or part thereof that is commonly used for
culinary (kitchen or edible) purposes." Believe it or not,
the word *vegetable* came into existence only about 200
years ago, since at that time all of our everyday vegetables were known as *herbs*—yes, even such commoners
as the Beet and Carrot. And until vegetables came into
use as we know them today, many were used years ago
as curative medicines, just as today these very ones are
so highly recommended by the medical laity as "protec-
tive foods" or "preventive medicines" without which
the various organs of our body cannot properly function.

A few examples: Lettuce leaves were eaten (or a
tea prepared) when a nerve sedative was needed, just as
today the green leaves of the Lettuce plant offer the various associated B vitamins, which doctors tell us will tend
to avoid and overcome nervous exhaustion. At one time,
the juice of boiled Asparagus and Beets, or an herbal
tea prepared of these two vegetables, was considered
an effective remedy for dropsy or kidney diseases; in this
case I am sure that quite a few of my fellow pharmacists have dispensed many prescriptions containing As-
paragin, which is the extract of our native Asparagus.
Onions and Garlic have been employed for hundreds of
years as effective remedies for "high blood pressure" and
asthmatic conditions, and today the medicinal efficacy
of these two herbs or vegetables has not lessened.

Let us remember too, that many of our familiar vegetables and fruits, as the Carrot, Onion, and Berries, were at one time wild plants and are descendants, so to speak, of the Wild Carrot (Queen Anne's Lace), the Wild Onion and wild Berries. These are the descendants, as Charles F. Saunders in his *Useful Wild Plants of the United States and Canada* stated nearly fifty years ago, "improved by cultivation and selection of ancestors as untamed in their way as the primitive men and women who first learned the secret of their nutritiousness."

Occasionally we may read in the newspapers and magazines thrilling articles and feature stories describing the practicability of employing as food many of the ubiquitous never-say-die herbs. Here are a few examples: "Wild Berries Only Food Until Man Found. J.B. was exhausted and hungry, but had been eating wild Strawberries. . ." "Plants with Edible Roots: Psoralea still is a favorite food of the plains Indians who dry it for a flour." (It is mentioned in the account of Lewis and Clark's and Fremont's travels.) . . . "Making Use of Native Shrub Fruits: The fruits of the High Bush Cranberry, Hawthorn and Rose are here recommended as ingredients for a syrup, sauce and jelly," which three are later described in the text. . . "Boy Lives Five Days on Diet of Grass: An 11-year old boy picked up by a car halfway between Jerusalem and Tel Aviv declared that he had lived for five days on nothing but grass." (And did Nebuchadnezzar, King of Babylon, eat grass or Alfalfa as did his oxen, because he wished to lose a few pounds of needless avoirdupois or to possibly heal a stomach ulcer?)

"Korean Diving Girls Expert Sea 'Gardeners': The diving girls search for food in the sea the year around. They bring up Seaweed, sea Cucumbers, sea Potatoes and even fish." . . . "Many Plants Termed Weeds Are Edible: A half-starved flier who was rescued after wan-

dering a week in Georgia's treacherous Okefenokee
Swamp was recovering today in Huey Hospital from
shock, exposure and minor injuries. The pilot, James
Douglas Stewart, of Weston, West Virginia, was reported in fairly good condition. He told doctors he ate
mushrooms and Bamboo shoots until found by three
Atlanta men camping in the swamp."

During World War II, in the early 40's, a course in
South Sea Island adaptation became part of the Ranger
and Combat School in Hawaii and, consisting as it did
of very practical and useful knowledge of the native
fauna and flora and invaluable means of quickly providing emergency food and shelter for our service-men, the
course became the "Castaway's Baedeker to the South
Seas." (Printed by the Objective Data Section, Intelli-
gence Center, Pacific Ocean Area, Pearl Harbor.) And
thus the student enrolled in this course became another
Robinson Crusoe and soon learned how to fare for himself in time of need on native foods. These included
Breadfruit, Bananas, Coconuts, Sugar Cane, Papayas,
Yams, and Almonds. A "millionaire's salad" was prepared from the soft white core within the base of the
sprouted coconut leaf and the marshmallow growth of
the meal of the fruit.

World hunger, which breeds revolution and unrest, could be
conquered if unusual foods, some of them considered weeds, were
more appreciated and utilized in the undeveloped countries, Prof.
Robert S. Harris of the Massachusetts Institute of Technology told
the American Academy of Arts and Sciences here.

Telling of his analysis of more than 1500 unusual food plants
in Mexico, Central America and China, Dr. Harris explained that
some people in the Mexican desert are well fed because they eat
native plants we would spurn, but which experience has taught
them can provide the essentials of good diet as well as meat, milk
and eggs which we consider necessary. Iron, calcium and needed
vitamins can be obtained from what we consider weeds.

For instance, malva* is a Mexican weed related to hollyhocks

*See Mallow

which would be promising material upon which plant breeders could work since it is a staple of Mexican Indians. Similarly a kind of laurel and a legume called chipilin are used as food successfully in Mexico.

Sweet potato leaves are another food that is used widely in Central America, Dr. Harris found. Good foods of this sort could be added to our diet and Americans could benefit from eating things that we have forgotten about or never knew could be eaten.

—News Report

In the War Department's official manual of emergency food plants and poisonous plants of the Pacific islands (TM 10-420), the following are listed among species that may be pressed into service to enable grounded fliers and "bushed" soldiers to live off the country, if need be: Ground Cherry, Black Nightshade, Water Chestnut, Dayflower, Seaside Morning-glory and Purslane—the latter more likely to be called "pussley" by fighters who were farmers a couple of years ago.

And furthermore, as a result of the shortages of fresh fruits during the war years, the need for the daily requirement of Vitamin C was adequately supplied by eating, uncooked, many herbs later described as *antiscorbutic* and the fruits of Wild Rose and Currants, et al, or drinking the infusions of their freshly gathered leaves.

Here are three further examples of desert plants that offer their edible portions in banquet style to all desert travelers: The Barrel Cactus, *Ferocactus acanthodes*, bears the well-earned title of "water-barrel" for it has been known to save the lives of many thirsty wanderers. To obtain its life-saving liquid, the top is cut off and its white, watery pulp is crushed with a stone and then squeezed by hand; and from the remaining pulp, delicious "candy" is made. The long bean pods of the fruitful mesquite, *Prosopis juliflora*, var. *glandulosa*, are gathered by the Indians of the Southwest in great quantities which are dried and ground and then put into their mush or soups. . . The fruits of the Giant Cactus, or the Saguaro, *Carnegiea gigantea*, are eaten in their fresh state by the Indians, who also extract the juice from the greater portion of their fruit crop to prepare a molasses-like syrup. And the seeds are also saved, dried and ground into a fine powder, and included when necessary in their mush.

A study of the stories behind these headlines would clearly demonstrate that there is nothing new to the eating of herbs. It has been done for centuries. Today, however, with the ever-increasing use of commercialized, nutritionless and foodless foods as white flour, carbonated beverages and canned foods, which inevitably give rise to and are accompanied by an equally ever-increasing rate of organic diseases, the consumption of nature-all foods as uncooked or cultivated fruits and vegetables and especially the herbal wildings has, to this day, fallen to and stayed at a very low level. Is there any wonder then, that 35 millions of Americans suffer needlessly with the more serious of the organic and incurable diseases as arthritis, diabetes and heart trouble? Diseased bodies and minds are the subsequent companion of so-called "civilized" foods, as witness the terrible, harmful effects on the children of the Filipinos and Maori, during the stay of their American benefactors.

This is further evidenced by a discussion of "Some Hopi Indian Foods" (which appeared in *The Herbarist*, a publication of the Herb Society of America) by George F. Carter, who wrote that "the impact of the superior white culture reinforced by habits taught by Indian Schools, together with the general decline of Indian culture, has tended to decrease the use of herbs (for food) by the younger people. It is the old folk who know the herbs and greens. The younger folk tend to be contemptuous of them and to turn instead to the white man's food such as white flour, canned goods, etc. This introduces a curious state of affairs, for in abandoning the old herbs, the youth are abandoning the food of their ancestors. From the probably vitamin-rich greens of their environs, to be had for the picking, they are turning to impoverished white flour and devitalized canned foods. And to get these, they must trade other things, including their own good corn."

"A few years ago," wrote Paul Hess, in *Health Culture*, " I had an opportunity to talk with the chief of the Cherokee Indians in western North Carolina. Upon questioning him as to the prevalence of cancer among his people, he informed me that only two cases had ever been known and these were reported within recent years. A gradual increase in the use of the white man's food (white flour, refined sugar, cookies, cakes, and other trashy foods bought in stores) together with drugs to palliate the resulting ailments will, no doubt, bring about, in time, a change for the worse in the health of the Cherokees. Among the Hopi Indians of the Southwest, cancer is said to be practically absent. Those people, despite the efforts of the government agriculturists to introduce modern farming methods, still raise and prepare their food in accordance with their traditional customs.

"The strength of the Chippewa in conquering the Sioux and establishing themselves in new territory indicates that they were well nourished, that suitable food was available, and that it was prepared in a proper manner. This was the work of the women, who were very industrious and bestowed much care on the provisioning of their households. A staple article of food was wild rice, which was seasoned with maple sugar or combined with broth made from ducks or venison. An important food value was obtained from maple sugar. Fish were extensively used, as the Chippewa, lacking horses, lived along the lakes and watercourses as much as possible. It is said that they had squash and pumpkins before the coming of the white man, and the country abounded in berries and wild fruit of many varieties. Thus it is seen that the Chippewa were a people subsisting chiefly on vegetable products and fish, though they secured deer and other animals by hunting. The making of gardens was an important phase of the industrial year, and a portion of the food thus obtained was stored in caches for winter use.

"Sometimes it is said that the privations of the North American natives, as to food supply, were due chiefly to the meagerness of the natural provisions that nature had for them, rather than to the neglect of these people to utilize and improve them. That this would be an unwarranted assumption appears when the variety and amount of vegetable food at their disposal is studied. Strange as it may seem, the list of plants that were used by the Indians and the early American settlers is long and varied. When they set out as pioneers in the wilderness, long before they were able to clear land and raise a crop to which they had been accustomed, they had to live upon the products of the land, which they knew by force of circumstances, rather than having learned it by rote from a book. Of the long list of natural plants that were available for human food, probably the most important ones were what are now known as herbs. There were the rose hips, the hawthorns, the partridge berries, the checkerberries, bark of trees, the wild onions, all of which are produced in abundance by nature. Included were all of the nuts from the nut trees inclusive of the oaks with their tremendous crops of acorns.

"It is a remarkable fact that before the advent of the white man, American Indians knew how to treat scurvy with substances rich in vitamin C at a time when effective antiscorbutics were unknown on the European continent except among Dutch country folk. In fact, when the second exploring expedition of Jacques Cartier up the St. Lawrence River was threatened with catastrophe from a severe epidemic of scurvy in 1535, it was saved through the use of an Indian remedy, a decoction of tree bark and leaves, probably from Sassafras. 'John Josselyn, Gent.' found, in his observations among the New England Indians in 1638, that these early Americans knew that cranberries 'are excellent against the Scurvy' and are good 'for the heat in Fevers' three centuries before scientists made the discovery that the berries possess a very high vitamin C content. Although the concept of vitamins in a strictly modern sense is very new, primitive man and civilization since antiquity have from time to time accidentally noted the therapeutic properties of vitamin foods and herbs, and have employed them extensively in the treatment of deficiency diseases."

"The Ojibwe," stated Huron H. Smith in his *Ethnobotany of the Ojibwe Indians*, are fond of their native foods, and since they regard all plants as the gift of their deities, and sacred to their uses, they feel that their native foods are medicine to keep them in health as well as foods. [*Ed.* Hippocrates, 500 B.C., had advised: "Let your foods be your medicine".] While they know nothing about vitamins or chemical constituents, they think that there are some salts or minerals in their native foods that keep them well. We know that they are correct in that. *They ascribe many of their present diseases to the abandonment of their native foods and the adoption of white men's foods. They think that the early failure of their teeth is due to using too much white flour for bread."* (My italics.)

However, there is one point that must be cleared up. That the Indians obtained most of their root vegetables and salad greens from the wild growing material, is the general conception, but this is far from the truth. Most of the tribes cultivated small gardens, or several patches, and these were invariably supervised by the woman of the household. In the gardens were found such crops as Beans, Beets, Carrots, Corn, Maize, Cabbage, Turnips. It is interesting to note, says Smith, that in the Indian's garden, one would "find garden flowers, and the lady of the house will be quite proud of them, and usually a little jealous of her neighbor if she has flowers that she has not."

Whenever friends mention to me that their gardens get so cluttered up with such "weeds" as Dandelion, Burdock or Lambsquarters, I say to them: "These weedy nondescripts may truly get on your horticultural nerves, and may become a bit rampant and take due advantage of the soil's richness or unmulched rows; but to discard as valueless many of these garden 'guests' or to avoid using them as a source of food or vegetable substitutes, is as unwise and uneconomical as depositing in the garbage disposal can a pound each of fresh Carrots and Celery."

Several seasons ago, a few of my neighbors maintained a large cooperative garden and I spent as much time in the process of "weeding" their respective sections of the garden as they did, yet I gathered no weeds per se: I had tangy salad greens and novel pot herbs and wholewheat flour substitutes for cookies and pancakes. You may smile with equal amazement and justified incredulity, not so much at my neighborliness in offering to help weed the various sections of my friends' gardens, but perhaps at my suggestions that they utilize these worthy herbs as food, which were not to be any more pooh-poohed at or discarded as worthless than the very produce which they were toiling so energetically to cultivate and nurse along. (Yes, seven years have passed and now they, too, are bona fide herb-eaters.)

I have described under Purslane the probability of the average gardener's failure to recognize the high food values of a most desirable vegetable substitute; and others like Lambsquarters, Mallow and Amaranth that are also discarded as "worthless." During World War

II, Victory gardeners were genuinely concerned with the appalling shortage of fresh foodstuffs. They who applied to practical use the priceless knowledge derived from federal and state agriculture or farmers' bulletins, which featured the desirability of garden weeds as food substitutes, are today the staunchest supporters of the "Eat The Weeds" program. (Undoubtedly the average no-herb-for-me gardener little realizes that most edible herbs are rarely troubled with the furtive acts of pheasants and rabbits, or with cutworms, plant lice, bean beetles and aphids.)

Let conservation be our main theme: Invariably, the neophyte herb-eater will have learned that his vast collection of dried edible leaves, seeds, nuts, berries— and many other herbs to be used as tea and coffee substitutes—will of course help him to win the constant battle against inflationary prices and also to save annually the cost of nearly 1000 gallons of gasoline. It certainly is an enviable pleasure to eat and not have to pay for the pleasure.

We have found that many gardeners, as a result of their practice of eating herbs, plan their vegetable gardens more thoughtfully, plant and tend them more zealously, harvest and store every Carrot, Potato and legume more faithfully than ever before. However, what is equally important is that our newly-found conservationist will have initiated a genuine economy in the kitchen. No longer are Radish, Turnip and Beet tops relegated to the garbage pail, for their nutritive values are at long last recognized, and now, Mrs. Housewife includes the greens of the first vegetable in a vegetable salad and steams those of the latter two a few minutes. Carrot tops are now cooked with all soups, chowders and stews. Orange, Tangerine and Lemon peels are now set aside, and when thoroughly dry, are ground and used as a seasoning herb or to infuse and enjoy as a refreshing caf-

feineless tea or coffe substitute. Dried cut Grapefruit
rinds are considered by the herbalist as "fruit quinine" of
which a warm drink is employed as a diaphoretic in
systemic colds. The rinds of all four may provide the
much needed ingredients for homemade jellies and preserves. The kitchen chemist will find that pickled Watermelon rinds are easy to prepare.

Other table discards will soon find their place in
such a planned economy: Dried Watermelon seeds are
now recommended by the medical laity in the treatment
of certain kidney and circulatory conditions; Squash
and Pumpkin seeds are used as worm expellants; Corn
silk is employed as a diuretic while the toothless cob is
finely cut and is applied, as should all vegetable waste,
as a mulch to the vegetable rows of one's garden. Also,
Sweet Potato leaves are a source of nourishing food that
is much used in Central America. Dr. Robert S. Harris
of the Massachusetts Institute of Technology found that
foods of this sort could be added to our diet and Americans could benefit from eating things that we have forgotten about or never knew could be eaten.

To provide a fairly constant supply of herb greens
throughout the Winter months, I will suggest that you
first gather the fully ripened seeds of such ever-present
stalwarts as Burdock, Shepherd's Purse, Dandelion and
Peppergrass, and after allowing them to dry a few days,
plant them in soil typical of their natural surroundings.
It is important that the window where you place the
flower pots have full sun. In a short time, you will be
presented with a dish of fresh salad greens. Any sprouted
Onions and Garlic should also be potted too, to provide
tangy, edible nutriment, as well as Chives, Parsley, and
the culinaries Sage, Thyme, and Lemon Balm.

Do not crowd the plants. Water the seeds and
young seedlings every day but not too much. Cut the

foliage down as needed for table use, or to prevent the plants from getting out of hand.

Herbs also provide the conservationist with food material for pet birds or poultry. A few of the more familiar herbs used for this purpose are Ragweed, Lambsquarters, Wild Caraway and Plantain.

Boy Scouts at Treasure Valley have tied a knot in the high cost of living. Scout chefs of Troop 165 cooked up a 5 course supper last night for the 12 members of the troop. It cost nothing. The only expenditure was time spent scouting the fields and forests of the mile-square reservation in search of edible plants and roots.

Housewives wishing to prepare such a non-cost meal have the following recipes to guide them.

Cow Lily Potatoes: These are roots of cow lily plants. Wash off muck before burying in live coals. Cook thoroughly to deaden marsh taste and serve hot.

Nettle Spinach: Leaves of stinging nettle plant cook quickly, like spinach, and make excellent green vegetable. Cook in boiling water and drain to get rid of poison from nettles. Rinse in hot water twice before eating.

Primrose Salad: Leaves should be thoroughly washed to avoid bugs in the salad.

Fruit Compote: Mix freshly-picked blueberries and wild raspberries. Add crushed wild mint leaves, 15 minutes before serving, stirring mixture.

Birch Tea: Made by steeping birch twigs and leaves in hot water.

Chicory Coffee: Roasted chicory roots are ground and boiled. Makes rather strong beverage.

Sumac Lemonade: Boil sumac twigs and leaves, then cool.

—News Report

The following passage is taken from Rackham Holt's excellent and factual biography* of Dr. George Washington Carver, late director of Agricultural Research of the Experimental Station at Tuskegee Institute, Alabama.

Dr. Carver was approached by a tramp one day

* *George Washington Carver.* Copyright 1943 by Doubleday and Co., Inc. Reprinted by permission.

who asked him for a dime for something to eat. As he
watched the tramp with the dime head for the nearest
store, he shook his head sadly.

"'It's pitiful, pitiful,' he said to his companion. 'Between here and that store there's enough food to feed a
town.' He pointed to the weeds growing beside the road
and to the wild plums overhead. 'And a balanced diet,
too.'

"It was uphill work persuading more than a handful
of the value of raising vegetables—of fighting King Cotton with such a puny weapon as logic.

"But Professor Carver hearkened to Isaiah, who
had hearkened to the Lord: 'The voice said, Cry. And
he said, What shall I cry?' Then the voice told him
what to say. 'All flesh is grass, and all the goodliness
thereof is as the flower of the field.' Isaiah had his ear to
the ground, and by listening Professor Carver heard also.
The voice said to him, go and get it, so he did.

"In most places, you had to put your foot down carefully as you stepped out the cabin door or it would crush
a cotton plant—and that meant crushing what represent-
ed money. But along the fence rows weeds sprouted
luxuriantly; and a wild vegetable by any other name
would taste as good.

"In their respective seasons Professor Carver had
for a long time included wild vegetables in his own diet
—clover tops, dandelion, wild lettuce, chicory, rabbit
tobacco, alfalfa, thistles, bed straw, pepper grass, wild
geranium, purslane and shepherd's purse. The dainty
chickweed which was pretty as to appearance and delicate as to taste, could be happily combined in salads or
stews, cold or hot. Curled dock made as good a pie as its
cultivated cousin, the rhubarb. From sour grass, or old-
fashioned sheep sorrel, he made not merely pies but confectionery and paint.

"A little earlier than asparagus in most localities,

the tender shoots of the pokeweed poked up through the soil. These were as delicate and delicious as the asparagus tips, which they resembled, as was also the swamp milkweed. Evening primrose, so pink as to be almost red, grew in masses.

"Lambsquarters, choicest of vegetables, was scattered over the temperate and subtropical sections of the country and was available from early until late summer. It made an immense amount of green stuff, was tender, crisp, and cooked easily. Before McCollum tested it on his rats and announced it contained the Fat Soluble A—one of the newly discovered and much-needed properties called 'Vitamines,' Professor Carver had proclaimed its high medicinal value.

"Most wild vegetables had a short season in which they were tender, but, being robust in flavor, they would keep well. The housewife could pack them in cans or jars and have shelves full of winter succulence. And, since jars were hard to come by for the really poor, they could be dried. That way they were practically imperishable, and required little storage place. Dehydrating wild vegetables seemed an excellent way to save the country's granary from the nibbling mice of waste."

* * *

One will admit that it is unusual to gather a basketful of edible herbs in a nearby field or empty lot with the same enthusiasm or confidence as when one purchases vegetables in the food mart; but is it any more unusual that some foods that are so commonplace to us were, until recently, a rarity in a country like England? One such example is Sweet Corn. In this respect, one news report stated: "The London newspapers today discovered that an intrepid English farmer is growing 1½ acres of sweet corn, which will go on sale for cob eating at 15 cents per ear, and one writer undertook to explain in this way: 'Corn is a favorite food in America, where it is grown largely in the southern states. It is also regarded as a great delicacy by Anglo-Indians throughout the east. The cob is boiled for 15 minutes and served like a potato in its jacket. The leaves are removed, butter or margarine is spread over the corn and it is sprinkled with pepper and salt. Then holding it at the ends, you nibble the corn like a rabbit.' " And—Sweet Corn is a member of the Grass family, as are Wild Oat and Wild Rice which abound in New England.

For many years, American research scientists and herbalists and certain organic gardeners have pointed out that Grass, whether it be highly prized blue Kentucky or the plain, everyday Massachusetts variety, is an all sufficient food, that Grass is equally as beneficial to Man as it is to animal, providing it is properly prepared so that it can be digested in sufficient quantities without difficulty.

Many drug stores sell a product that is eaten together with meals by convalescents and others suffering with anemia and this product consists solely of powdered ordinary green, garden grass. Other grass products include an edible flake mixture and compressed tablets of grass and vegetables and a host of much overrated chlorophyllized products as toothpaste, personal deodorants, etc.

"England is prepared to use grass for food if supplies run low," said Professor D. B. Johnstone-Wallace of Cornell University during World War II. He told the Canadian Institute of Public Affairs in 1942 that large factories were already producing dried grass powder and it was being fed to animals. "It will soon be fed to human beings if they are wise," he added. Johnstone-Wallace has eaten grass himself, mixed half-and-half with flour and baked into soda biscuits. "Green grass is nutritious and tastes really fine," he said.

You still don't welcome the thought of eating grass?

Then, pray tell, why at breakfast do you eat farina or oatmeal or wheat germ grains (or even toast, for that matter)? These cereals are members of the grass family and others more familiar to us (out of 1000 assorted relatives) include Bamboo, sweet Corn, Sugar Cane, Barley, Oat and Rice.

Does the eating of grass or weeds or herbs seem strange to those accustomed to store-bought produce? Does the writer's habit of drinking a warm tea of freshly cut and quick dried grass also seem strange to the uninitiated? Then do remember that young grass is one of Nature's richest sources of composite food nutrients. There is besides that much ballyhooed chlorophyll, a high content of Vitamin A and C, five factors of Vitamin B complex, K and G. It has been estimated that 12 pounds of powdered grass contain more vitamins than 340 pounds of vegetables and fruits—more vegetables and fruits than the average person can eat a year. (Please note that although vitamins per se were unknown in biblical days, the prophet Jeremiah observed that certain organic diseases were due to mineral-vitamin deficiency: "Their eyes did fail, because there was no grass" (14:6).

Dr. Charles F. Schnabel, formerly of Rockhurst College, Kansas City, believed that "the time is not far off when we'll be consuming a daily portion of grass in butter, bread, milkshakes, candy bars, breakfast foods, pancakes, and even ice cream and cookies." He stated that by mixing dried grass to the daily diet, the annual food bill could be cut at least 25% and place a rounded-out diet in reach of everyone's pocketbook.

Had Dr. Schnabel's job as a mill feed chemist held out in the depression, grass as a human diet supplement might not be a scientific factor today. But 1931 found him hard hit for money to feed his family. He yielded to an urge to try his family on the grass that had put his small flock of chickens to producing eggs on an al-

most 100 per cent basis for five months. By adding dehydrated grass to the family's menu he nourished the
eight on a dollar a day—12 cents apiece. Today his
children all are proportionately larger than their father.
To have a constant supply of grass at the right stage, he
space-planted his two-acre plot at the edge of town on a
two-week interval plan. Four o'clock every morning
found him cutting grass. He quick dried it over the hot
air registers of his home. Then the grass was ground in a
sausage-grinder and put in the family's milk. Sometimes
when the temperature was 80 degrees outside, the Schnabel furnace was running full blast. Mrs. Schnabel ad-
mits now she wouldn't like to go through the hot register
process again but she adds, "Every woman who marries
a scientist must expect such things."

"They are living proof," Schnabel says of his children, "of the benefits of grass as a food. I've fed them
grass for 11 years. Look at them. Not a decayed tooth
in their heads. The only sicknesses they've known have
been a few common child diseases."

Dr. W.R. Graham, of Ontario, Canada, worked on
"gray hair factor" in grass research. He found black
mice got gray hair if they were denied grass vitamins.
He does not say that grass will cure gray hair in humans.
The B Vitamins are known to have some role in keeping
natural color in hair.

Mrs. Moore-Pataleena, of London, England, has
a startling recipe for sustenance, health and youthful-
ness. She finds plenty to eat wherever she goes, which
costs her nothing. She doesn't contend with shopping
lines, but does with inclement and wintry weather. Says
she: "I have been eating grass for six years and I'm getting younger every day. When the grass is tender, I
eat it whole; if it's tough I grind it and extract the juice,
or cook it." Some 16 years after a pilgrimage to the Hima-
layas, Mrs. Moore-Pataleena began to spurn convention-

al foods, and lived on raw fruits and vegetables and during the war years turned to grass and edible "weeds." And she adds: "I also drink small amounts of honeyed water, eat a few nuts or freshly ground carrot or fruit, but mostly I rely on grass. And," smiled the 55-year-young naturalist, "I expect to live to be 200."

* * *

"Green scum on ponds," said *Horticulture*, "which used to be regarded as an indication of stagnant water and of 'dog days' seems to have been underestimated by the public. This stuff, or some of its cousins among the algae, may eventually solve many human problems —including the universal one of getting enough to eat. It is believed that future human populations may be kept from starving by production of improved strains of algae, capable of being processed into high-protein food. These one-celled plants, it seems, are nature's most efficient device for capturing the sun's energy and turning it into hydrocarbons, or for taking nitrogen and other elements and manufacturing proteins. Lacking the wasteful stems, roots and leaves of higher plants, algae are almost all food. Dried algae cells have been found to be more than half protein. Algae culture is done in water which has been fertilized to supply the necessary nutritional elements and compounds that cannot be drawn from air and pure water. The alga *Chlorella* was used in experiments at Cambridge, Mass., and elsewhere by the Carnegie Institution. It is said to have a 'vegetable-like flavor, resembling raw lima beans or raw pumpkin.' "

"He causeth the grass to grow for the cattle, and herbs for the service to man; that he may bring forth food out of the earth."—*Psalm 104*

*A Few Examples of the Vitamins and Minerals of the
    Native Herbs*

Vitamins

A—Alfalfa, Clover, Dandelion, Watercress.

B—Alfalfa, Blueberry Leaves, Burdock, Wild Rice,
    Watercress.

C—Burdock Seeds, Dandelion, Horseradish, Milkweed,
    Mustard Leaves, Pokeweed, Rose Hips, Shepherd's
    Purse, Skunk Cabbage, Sorrel, Watercress.

D—Watercress.

E—Dandelion, Wild Oats, Watercress.

K—Alfalfa, Chestnut Leaf, Grass, Shepherd's Purse.

P—Rose Hip (fruit).

Minerals

Calcium—Bedstraw, Chamomile, Chives, Coltsfoot,
    Dandelion, Horsetail, Meadowsweet, Nettle, Plan-
    tain, Shepherd's Purse, Sorrel, Toadflax.

Chlorine—Nearly all plants contain Chlorine in combina-
    tion with Sodium.

Iodine—Iceland Moss, Irish Moss, Kelp, Sarsaparilla.

Iron—Burdock, Meadowsweet, Mullein, Nettle, Straw-
    berry Leaf, Toadflax, Yellow Dock.

Magnesium—Meadowsweet, Mullein, Evening Prim-
    rose, Toadflax, Walnut, Willow Bark.

Phosphorus—Caraway, Chickweed, Sweet Flag, Mari-
    gold, Meadowsweet, Sorrel, Watercress.

Potassium—Birch Bark, Borage, Chamomile, Colts-
    foot, Dandelion, Doggrass, Fennel, Sweet Flag, Mul-
    lein, Nettle, Oak Bark, Peppermint, Plantain, Wal-
    nut, Yarrow.

Silicon—Burdock, Horsetail, Skunk Cabbage.

Sodium—Bedstraw, Fennel, Meadowsweet, Nettle,
    Shepherd's Purse, Black Willow.

Sulphur—Burdock, Coltsfoot, Fennel, Sweet Flag, Mea-
    dowsweet, Mullein, Nettle, Plantain, Shepherd's
    Purse, Skunk Cabbage.

TABLE OF AVERAGE NUTRIENT VALUES OF EDIBLE HERBS

	Food Energy	Protein	Fat	Carbohydrate	Calcium	Phosphorus	Iron	Vitamin A	Thiamin (Vit. B)	Riboflavin	Niacin	Ascorbic Acid (Vitamin C)
	Cal.	Gm.	Gm.	Gm.	Mg.	Mg.	Mg.	I.U.	Mg.	Mg.	Mg.	Mg.
Amaranth	36	3.5	.5	6.5	267	67	3.9	6090	.08	.16	1.4	80
Blackberries (fresh)	57	1.2	1.0	12.5	32	32	.9	200	.04	.04	.04	21
Blueberries	61	.6	.6	15.1	16	13	.8	280	.02	.02	.30	16
Burdock	94	3.1	.1	6.8	26	60	1.0	310	.06	.12	.5	72
Chives	42	3.8	0.6	7.8	76	91	2.5	500	.11	–	–	59
Coriander	36	2.5	0.4	7.3	169	60	5.9	5940	.10	.12	1.0	83
Cranberries	48	.4	.7	11.3	14	11	.6	40	.03	.02	0.1	12
Currant (red)	55	1.2	0.2	13.6	36	33	.9	120	.04	–	–	36
Dandelion (greens)	44	2.7	0.7	8.8	187	70	3.1	13650	.19	.14	.8	38
Fennel	28	2.8	0.4	5.1	100	51	2.7	3500	–	–	–	31
Horseradish	87	3.2	.3	19.7	140	64	1.4	–	.07	–	–	81
Lotus Root	49	1.7	.1	11.3	21	74	0.4	–	.05	–	–	22
Mustard (greens)	22	2.3	.3	4.0	220	38	2.9	6460	.09	20.	0.8	102
Peppergrass	41	4.2	1.4	5.3	211	38	2.9	2970	.11	.17	1.0	87
Raspberries, (black)	57	1.2	.4	13.8	40	37	.9	130	.02	.07	.3	24
Rice, wild (raw)	26	1.2	.2	5.5	5	36	.6	red –	.09	.04	.2	2
Strawberries	37	.8	.5	8.3	28	27	.8	60	.03	.07	.3	60
Walnut	654	15.	64.4	15.6	83	380	2.1	30	.48	.13	1.2	3
Watercress	18	1.7	.3	3.3	195	46	2.0	4720	.08	.16	.8	77

Identifying the Herbs

We have already mentioned that a large variety of edible herbs are to be found in everyone's vegetable garden, but which "weed" is what edible herb? Thus the following procedure is recommended to the novice: Every day, collect one or two specimens of each unknown herb, and press and dry them so as to preserve as well as possible the original likeness and color. Include enough of the plant to show entire leaves, flower and if possible, the fruit. Note on your card or paper holding the specimens the date and place of collection. Number each specimen with a tag and keep a duplicate for further reference. Pack each dried specimen first between paper, then cardboard, and put your name and address on the package. Now you are ready to have these specimens identified for you.

Identifiers include the following:

Curators of Museums of Natural History.

Botany and science teachers of high schools and colleges.

Farm folks.

The grandparents and the older folks at home.

The personnel of the State Extension Service and experimental stations of Agricultural Colleges.

Practicing herbalists.

* * *

"The best doctors in the world are Doctor Diet, Doctor Quiet, and Doctor Merryman."—*Jonathan Swift*

Collection and Preservation

Collection of the Herbs

The time for collecting or the season of availability of the herbs is mentioned under each herb. It will be noted by the experimenter that a few herbs come under the category of "whenever available" as do young or early Trefoil, Chickweed and Hollyhock. Thus, although the general rule provides for the gathering of greens during the Spring to early Summer season these three may be gathered and used as late as December.

To afford oneself with an almost continual supply of nutriment-laden greens during the winter months, one should gather quantities of seeds of the more prolific growers such as Burdock, Dandelion, Milkweed and Evening Primrose. Plant the seeds in rich but not over-composted soil, contained in flower-pots, indoor window boxes, or even in decorated tin cans.

Mention is made in the text regarding the forcing of certain root herbs, as with Poke, Skunk Cabbage, Wild Garlic and Onion. Experience will teach one to abandon the practice of forcing the former two indoors— and usually in one's cellar—if only because the grown shoots are generally blanched and therefore devoid of optimum nutrients. With the latter two, the method recommended is to separate and force the cloves, say of Garlic (wild or cultivated), in organically healthy soil, and the resultant greens may then be included preferably uncooked in salads or cole slaw, or when diced, to add

extra food value or to season a spread of cottage cheese
and soured cream.

Drying and Preservation of the Herbs

Throughout the text, the following phrases appear
rather frequently and refer to the preservation in the dry
state of scores of edible herbs which Nature provides in
welcome abundance: "Dehydrate any excess and save
for future meals. . ." "Dry and save for future use,
in jams, jellies, etc." We may have collected a basketful
too much of Dandelion or Burdock leaves, or an amount
far in excess of what we may consume within the next
day or two; thus we should save and use the dried and
ground leaves in soups or stews as later described.

To dehydrate and save for future use, tie with
string the stems of whole herbs and suspend as near as
possible to the ceiling, preferably in a warm and well
(fresh) air-circulated attic, or in the hallway next to
the kitchen. It is always important to preserve their natural appearance, and thus their food values, by keeping
the herb bunches *away from the direct sunlight*. Such
leaves as the finely textured Sassafras and Amaranth
may be allowed to dry on the attic floor or on improvised
racks, but should be turned over occasionally. Dry flowers and seeds on trays of chicken screening or cheesecloth. Above all: *Do not crowd the drying material*.

When the herbs (leaves) are thoroughly dried,
they are finely ground and stored in air-tight glass jars.
Store dried fruit, nuts and flowers in their natural state.

To use the dried leaves as food, allow the dry
material to soak in cold water 10 to 15 minutes, wash
again with cold water and strain. Dried (dehydrated)
fruits should soak at least 6 to 8 hours.

Note: Although some vitamin content will inevitably be destroyed during the dehydrating process, very
little of the more important minerals will be lost.

For further information, see Bulletin No. 404,

"Home Dehydration of Vegetables," Massachusetts Agricultural Experiment Station, Amherst, Massachusetts.

Freezing the Herbs

We may thank Clarence Birdseye's pioneering efforts of the 1920's for accomplishing the first commercial freezing of fish. From 1927 on, quick-freezing was extended to fruits and vegetables and freezing became a major process of food preservation.

I still recall Grandfather's storage cellar. This takes me back some 50 years to World War I days when I attended the Roger Walcott grammar school. Grandfather's was rather a sub-cellar room, of about 8' x 8' dimensions, actually dug out below the surface of the house cellar. It was high enough for me, and on "tippity-toes" I could just about touch the ceiling of that room, whereas Grandfather and all other grown-ups had better duck down a bit or else. . . . One had to be quite light-footed and as poised as a ballet dancer to get from the cooling herbed wines and vinegars on one side to the other, to the ice-cold or near-frozen Shallots, Beans, fruits and weedy herbs, Radishes and other vegetables directly across.

The refrigeration? A large 2' x 5' slab of ice placed in a dug-out hole and covered with straw and cardboard. We sure needed a coat or sweater going into the ice cellar, it was that cold!

But these days, home freezing as a method of preserving herbal foods is becoming more and more accepted. It helps to insure the fresh tangy flavor and the much needed health-fortifying nutrients — if the herbs, as well as other table vegetables and fruits, are eaten within a reasonable length of time.

The freezing of the weedy edibles takes nearly the same format and cautions that pertain to the freezing of our garden produce—Peas, Beans, Berries, et al—and requires very little work or time.

(We have discovered that our wild-growing or garden produce, properly stored, kept better and tasted better than store-bought frozen items, if only for this reason — no processing, no heating, and no adding of dangerous chemicals and synthetic dyes.)

The freezing of tender Lettuce-like leaves is not recommended, but for home use, quickly-blanched tops of Beets, Turnips, and Spinach may be frozen.

And now a few examples of freezable herbs:

Cattails: The inner leading shoots of the rootstalks are collected and stored in Autumn and throughout Winter. When needed they are included in a fresh salad or steamed with other vegetables. (Be sure to permit complete thawing.)

Purslane, Japanese Knotweed and Lambsquarters: They are washed and stored as is. Allow 5 minutes of steaming.

Wild Onion and Wild Garlic: As above.

Early leaves of Dandelion, Chicory, Nettles, Yellow Dock and Burdock with or without roots: Require 7-10 minutes of steaming.

Upper tops of Peppergrass and *young* Wintercress: May later be included in salad or soup.

Milkweed: The early shoots minus the bottom inch of white and the bonodorous, purple flowers are either steamed or included in soup.

See also Blueberries and Cranberries.

—Wash quickly, or spray with *cold* water, leaf and seed herbs before freezing them.

—Be sure to freeze any excess of ground peels of Orange, Lemon, Lime and Tangerine and have them ready as seasoners for cakes and pastries, breads and stuffings, and for fish and meats.

—Use only such fruits as are in perfect condition and not overripe. Berries may harden like marbles but won't stick together.

—The sooner the foods are placed in the freezer after picking, the better the product.

—Freezing keeps the food from losing moisture and protects its nutrient values, flavor and color.

—Herbs that will be consumed within 15-20 days should be refrigerated; all others may be frozen.

—Before storing any food in the freezer, first remove any ice nearing the space-wasting ½ inch thickness.

—Store the items at a maximum of 0° Fahrenheit; the lower the better, of course.

—Use bags (and sheets) of non-rigid, moisture-vapor-resistant packaging material, cellophane or polyethylene, etc. They are filled easily, and upon thawing, the food is readily removed. The packages must be airtight and moisture-proof.

—Sealing the package makes it leak-proof and protects the food from absorbing and giving off odor and flavor.

—The bags stack well in the freezer and require little space. File them alphabetically.

—Once green herbs or fruits are removed from the refrigerator or freezer, they must be used.

Modus Preparandi

If one is to get the most out of the edible herbs, which, as will be shown, do contribute their full share to a much more alkaline-balanced diet, one must apply the same careful rules to their preparation for table use as to garden cultivated foods. Poor preparation, specifically over-cooking, not only tenderizes and discolors greens especially, but what is by far more important, the health-restoring minerals and vitamins are ever being deposited in the pot-liquor which, under the usual procedure of preparing vegetables, contains far more of the nutrients than food recently cooked and which is too often discarded as waste. (Indeed, it would be far better generally to discard the cooked vegetables and drink the pot-liquor.) Whatever vegetable juice is left over as "liquor" should be saved, sweetened or disguised, and later served as a vegetable cocktail. The conservationist will do well to include such leftover vegetable (or herb) juices in a later soup.

In readying the freshly collected herbs for table use, these rules should be adhered to:

1. Collect only as much as is needed for the day's meals.

2. Remove all dried leaves, coarse stalks and adhering soil.

3. Wash twice with cold water only and allow to drain.

4. Store in a cool place or refrigerator.

5. Use as soon as possible or prepare immediately before mealtime.

Processing

Uncooked: Whenever possible, eat the herbs as uncooked greens alone or in a salad combination with other herbs or vegetables, seasoned gently with herb vinegar and salad oil. A clove of garlic (Yes, why not of wild Garlic?) previously rubbed juicily and judiciously over the salad bowl will add extra zest to the salad or cole slaw.

Steaming: 1. This method requires the least amount of water and heat and obviously prevents further waste of the valuable nutrients.

2. Utensils of stainless steel, glass or porcelain are recommended in that order.

Note: *To boil is to spoil.* Do not overcook vegetables, for long cooking produces a flat, tasteless flavor, destroys much of the natural color and ends up with a needless loss of much-needed nutrients. Save the pot-liquor for a vegetable cocktail or soup.

Do not use soda when preparing greens or vegetables.

If you are to use frozen foods—herbs can be so preserved—start the cooking while they are still frozen and serve them as soon as they've thawed.

Herb Powder

There are many leaves and seeds that dry and powder well, and in powdered form may be employed in three ways: as a coarse powder, to become an ingredient in pastries or pancakes, to season a salad dressing, or to sprinkle over a soup or stew; or as a fine powder to yield a salt substitute with which to season warm or cooked foods; and as a capsulated supplement, substituting for a vitamin capsule.

1. Of course, any of the dried greens may be used when preparing a soup or stew. They are first coarsely cut or ground and added to the warming food in the last few minutes of preparation. The finely ground or powdered herb may also be added to cole-slaw, creamed or cottage cheese, to a salad dressing or sauce and to blended products.

As the chief ingredient of cookies and bread, we have employed the fruits (seeds) of Wild Buckwheat, Barnyard Grass, and Foxtail, leaves and seeds of Amaranth, and Lambsquarters and Masterwort, plus those listed below. And they do equally as well for soups and stews, stuffings, and for chicken and fish patties.

2. To prepare a salt substitute, the cut herbs are powdered via a Molinex or similar coffee mill—even a meat grinder will do—and sifted through a sieve or through several layers of cheese cloth, thus removing the coarse stems and stubborn leaf portions.

The herbs:
Wild Carrot leaves
Yellow Dock fruits
Goldenrod leaves
Lambsquarters fruits
Masterwort leaves
Nettle leaves
Peppergrass leaves and fruits
Peppermint leaves
Sassafras leaves and bark
Shepherd's Purse leaves and fruits
Spearmint leaves
Tansy leaves (young)

You may use whatever other herbs you find will powder well.

Similarly, a powder may be obtained from such usually discarded valuables as (dried) leaf tops of Carrots, Beets, Radish, et al, and mixed with the above powder.

Formula:

    1 Tablespoonful of the above powder

    2 Tablespoonsful of Kelp (Seaweed)

    1-4 Teaspoonsful of powdered aromatic herbs—
        Basil, Celery Seed, Dill Seed, Marjoram,
        Thyme, Savory. (Any two or more of your
        choice)

    Mix all together.

    Label: Ingredients and date of preparation.

Use as a salt substitute instead of the harmful salt and pepper, for soups, stews, omelettes, meats, fish, etc.

    3. Food Supplement.

Use any combination of the above powdered herbs, especially Nettle, Wild Carrot and Lambsquarters. For this purpose use *no* culinary herbs or Kelp.

Purchase 100 empty Lilly Co. #00 gelatin capsules from your druggist. (Cost is approximately $1.60; per thousand about $10.00.)

Separate the capsule parts. Tap the larger part onto the powder until no more is taken up. Into the smaller part, insert only enough powder to cover the rounded bottom. Then push together the two parts of the capsule until they fit snugly.

The dose: One capsule 3 times a day at mealtime.

Juicing the Herbs

This is an excellent way for the herb user and health enthusiast to employ just-gathered, native herbs and home-grown vegetables. Their freshly expressed juices provide us with a "quick lunch" or a slow drink.

Alan, son #4, and I had for several years (until he reached his junior year at high school) made a practice of having "green refreshments" after our workout in the garden. We would take 3 or 4 handfuls of freshly mown green grass plus the leaves of that Dandy Lion and his front-lawn neighbors, Sour Grass, Burdock and Chickweed. Or from the garden patch in our backyard these notables were enlisted — Yellow Dock, Hollyhock, Lambsquarters, and others whom we encountered on our way to the kitchen. A drink (5-6 ounces) of these herbal friends — Alan would sweeten his with a little honey — would sustain us for several hours and often during the Summer months constituted for us and Brother Herbert a liquid lunch.

Buy whichever juicer is your desire and within your price range. Do make sure that it is rust-proof 100% stainless steel wherever the fresh juice touches the apparatus.

Note: One such daily cupful of herbed juice is of inestimable value to the health-watcher, the weight-reducer, and to all who seek this highly chlorophyllated nectar of Mother Nature's own garden-laboratory.

—*Eat* the liquid slowly: Swish a *small amount* about in the mouth before swallowing. This insures the liquid being thoroughly mixed with the enzymes of the saliva.

—The beginner should mix ½-¼ cup of herbed juice with ½-¾ cup of vegetable juice according to taste. *Just enough* honey may be added to sweeten. But molasses?

—The herbs: Green Grass, Alfalfa, Watercress, leaves of Yellow Dock, Dandelion, Purslane, and Grape; Burdock leaves and stems, Peppergrass, Lambsquarters, Amaranth and Japanese Knotweed, and others of your choice.

—Complementary vegetables: Parsley, Celery, greens of Turnip and Beets, Kale, Romaine Lettuce, Cabbage, Spinach, Carrot and Greens.

—Fruits: Wild Cherries (minus seeds), Grapes, Rose Hips, Blueberries, Raspberries. Use with Apples, Pears, and Dates. And no sweetening, honey or sugar.

—A fruit drink must be taken alone and constitutes a complete meal, preferably breakfast. Do not drink such liquids between meals, the better to provide complete digestion of the previous meal.

—Cranberries, Currants, Strawberries are acid fruits and therefore taken only with Orange, Lemon or Grapefruit.

—To prepare the juice, all items are first quickly washed (roots and stems require brushing). Absorb excess water with towel. Put leaves in first, stems next, and roots last.

—The resultant juice yields 85-90% of the nutritional elements, is easily digested and assimilated by the blood stream within 30-40 minutes.

Do *not* mix together juices of fruits and vegetables. Drink each separately.

—Drink the prepared juice only if freshly expressed and as needed. Do not store.

Blending the Herbs, via a Blender

This is an excellent way of using the herbs of your choice or those mentioned under *Juicing the Herbs.* These commoners have been much used to great advantage by the members of the herb-study classes: Green Grass, stems of Burdock and Japanese Knotweed, Mints and a little Catnip, Watercress and the early rosettes of Evening Primrose.

Be sure to wash well the herbal parts with cold water immediately before blending. Before partaking of this preparation, dilute each ⅓ cupful of processed herbs with ⅓ or ⅔ water. Stir well, mix carefully with saliva before sipping small amounts of the liquid. Season with culinary herbs or salt substitute to taste.

Such blended herbs may be incorporated with creamed or cottage cheese to prepare a variety of spreads, and with salad dressings, etc.

Prepare only when needed. Do not store.

Vinegared Items

To flavor a vinegar, these herbs may be used either alone or in combination: Wild Ginger root, Pennycress, Shepherd's Purse, Checkerberry, Wild Allspice, Masterwort root and seeds, early Tansy leaves, Catnip, Pennyroyal, Wormwood, Mints, Bayberry leaves, Wild Onion and Wild Garlic, Sweet Flag root, and Horseradish root.

And, of course, the never-to-be-discarded peels of Orange, Lemon, Lime and Tangerine.

Except for Horseradish, most of these aromatics may also be used to flavor commercial or home-made wines.

The vinegar to use: Malt or cider or wine; never white distilled.

To aromatize this item, do not use pure vinegar. Do use a standard formula of *diluted* vinegar.

The herbs to be vinegared (a few examples):

The young 4-5 inch tops and roots of Wild Carrot and Burdock.

The white, inner portions of Cattail's lower stem.

Roots of young Solomon's-seal, both varieties, and Jerusalem Artichoke.

The flower buds of the early Marsh Marigold.

Whole herbs of Wild Onion and Garlic, Purslane, and Live Forever.

Small, young Mushrooms.

I recall that Grandfather prepared our pickles not only with short Cukes but with Cauliflower and small green Tomatoes as well.

Also into other vinegars, the result of his allowing his herb wines to sour, went other such favorites which should be included in the above list — the green, unripe Barberries, Crab Apples, and Cranberries which

the Harris children would collect on many a Fall week-
end in the Lower Dorchester bogs, the Nasturtium seeds,
Radishes and Leeks of our garden, and dozens of weedy
nondescripts.

One familiar with any of the above listed edibles
may soon learn to prepare many differently flavored
vinegars.

Season each vinegar with whatever herbs
are available and plentiful.

Do use various combinations of aromatics
and note the difference.

Use a wide-mouthed jar. Label the jar
with date and ingredients.

To a cupful of coarsely ground seasoning
herbs, add a quart of slightly warmed vinegar
and shake well. Let stand in a warm place
10-14 days. Shake the jar gently every day.

(Note: Such herbed vinegars may be employed in salad dressings,
alone or wth oil for a vegetable salad and as a marinating
or basting solution).

Save — save the jars containing the pickling liquid
of store-bought pickles. To this add a tablespoonful of
herbal vinegar, roots, fruits and seeds, plus cut Carrots,
Celery, Cauliflower, and whatever else you think worth
pickling.

Native Herbs used as Food Seasoners

Herb	Part Used	Preparation
Wild Allspice	Fruits	Vinegar, coarse meat
Angelica	Leaves, roots, seeds	Soup, stew, starchy vegetables
Bayberry	Leaves	Soup, stew, salt substitute
Sweet Birch	Leaves and twigs	Vinegar, soup
Wild Carrot	Seeds, leaves	Salt substitute, soup, fish
Catnip	Leaves and flowers	Sauce, substitute for peppermint
Chamomile	Leaves and flowers	Cooked cabbage and broccoli
Sweet Clover	Leaves, flowers, fruits	Soup, stew, powder
Sweet Flag	Roots	Fish, meat, substitute for ginger or cinnamon
Wild Garlic	Whole plant	Soup, salad dressing, sauce
Wild Ginger	Root	Vinegar, substitute for ginger
Horseradish	Root	Vinegar, soup, stew, coarse meat and fish
Juniper	Fruits	Vinegar, soup, stew, venison
Masterwort	Leaf stalks, roots, seeds	Soup, stew, cooked vegetables
Mountain Mint	Whole plant	Substitute for other mints
Nasturtium	Whole plant, seeds	Salad, pickle
Wild Onion	Whole plant, seeds	Soup, dressing, sauce
Peppergrass	Leaves and fruits	Herb salt, soup, stew, salad, vinegar
Peppermint	Whole plant	Jelly, soup, lamb, potato
Sassafras	Leaves, bark	Soup, stew, cooked vegetables, vinegar
Sheep's Sorrel	Whole plant	Salad, cole slaw, puree
Shepherd's Purse	Whole plant	Herb salt, soup, stew, salad
Spearmint	Whole plant	See under peppermint
Tansy	Young leaves	Substitute for sage, vinegar, cookies
Wormwood	Leaves and flowers	Vinegar, discreet substitute for tarragon
Watercress	Leaves	Salad

Sprouted Seeds

What to do with the hundreds, nay thousands, of herb seeds which we collect in the Fall? Why, sprout a few of them, thus again offering us an abundance of a concentrated food supply throughout the Fall-Winter-Spring months. And when we crave "garden fresh" greens, we turn to our window garden.

Poor Mrs. Harris! Every sunshiny window shelf (except one spared for her Japanese rubber plants, Begonias and African Violets) is ever taken up with my sprouting seeds and mini-herbs and Garlic green-sprouts. The services of all windows—from the utility room and dining room and living room to the three bedrooms upstairs and the den — have been enlisted to sprout-sprout-sprout, whether for immediate consumption or for later transplanting into the garden.

The soil method of sprouting differs from water sprouting of Mung, Lentils or Soy beans, in that a regular sprouter or other acceptable apparatus is employed to greatly lessen the duration of sprouting activity. Sprouts are ready in 3 to 6 days. Use such food seeds as Rye, Corn, Barley, Peas, Lentils, and the everyday assortment of Beans such as Lima, Fava, et al. This method requires that the sprouting seeds be kept in a warm and *dark* area.

You may use this quick method of producing sprouts but we have grown our herb seeds in both rich and poor sandy soil or a mixture of both, or in a combination soil, gravel, sand and vermiculite, and in the latter alone. We still use all kinds of unconventional containers for speed sprouting: All shapes and sizes of flower pots, small and shallow pans and containers, and vegetable boxes, etc.

Every sprouted seed offers us in concentrated form the particular multi-minerals, vitamins and enzymes of the mature plants, factors that are complete and organic.

Sprouted seeds activate the precursors of Vitamins C
and A and offer an excellent supply of the daily requirement of Vitamins B and E. The Vitamin C herein provided is the anti-scurvy factor and is easily assimilated
by the blood stream, for which reason alone one should
eat daily portions of sprouted Peas, Beans, Dandelion
and other herbs.

The Seeds:

Alfalfa	Fenugreek
Amaranth	Wild Garlic
Barley	Lambsquarters
Burdock	Wild Onion
Wild Carrot	Parsley
Clover (Red,	Peppergrass
Yellow, White)	Plantain
Dandelion	Radish
Yellow Dock	Sesame (unhulled)
	Sunflower

Buy the seeds from an organic gardener or seed
producer. Make sure that the seeds intended for sprouting are viable (i.e. capable of developing) and free
from chemical treatment. Those intended for human
consumption (for table use) and sold in the grocery
markets are not always viable.

Use the seedlings as an extra ingredient in the
juicer or blender, in salads and with steamed vegetables,
and over soups and stews.

Tisane

A tisane is an herb tea, or better a health tea, intended as a substitute for Tea or Coffee. It should be
drunk by all, and especially by one who may be suscep-
tible to the dyspepsiating tannic acid and the insidious
over-stimulation of the caffeine of these two undesirable
beverages.

A warm herb tea will keep one cool in the Summer

and more comfortable in the Winter, and those who require a refresher or a mildly aromatic after-dinner drink will certainly derive much comfort and pleasure from a "Northern Julep" of Mint and Sage.

1. Rinse cup and saucer with hot water before adding the herbs, previously dried and ground.

2. Stir well one heaping teaspoonful of dry herbs in a cup of boiled water and keep saucered about 5-7 minutes.

3. Stir and strain. Add Lemon or honey as desired.

Note: a. Always prepare a fresh cup of herb tea.

b. Always drink warm. Iced teas are therapeutically inert and therefore not recommended.

Use These Culinary Herbs:

Anise, Bee Balm, Lemon Balm, Basil, Bergamot, Costmary, Fennel, Rose Geranium, Hyssop, Lavender, Marjoram, Rosemary, Sage, Thyme, Lemon Verbena.

And The Native Herbs:

Alfalfa, Angelica, Caraway, Catnip, Chamomile, Checkerberry, Fennel, Sweet Fern, Sweet Goldenrod, Linden, Peppermint, Raspberry, Sassafras, Spearmint, Strawberry, Wintergreen, Yarrow.

Note: The dried ground peel of Lemon, Orange, and Tangerines should also be added.

Examples of a Few Herb Teas and Their Uses

Herbs	Uses
Alfalfa and Mint	Sources of Vitamins A, D, E, K. Minerals, Calcium, Iron, Manganese
Lemon Balm	Used to flavor fruit drinks
Chamomile	Calmative, digestant
Linden and Mint	Anti-Dyspeptic
Catnip and Fennel	Carminative
Sage and Catnip	"Cold Breaker"
Sage and Peppermint	"Northern Julep"

Rose Petals	Source of Vitamin C, Minerals, Magnesium, Calcium and Iron
Basil, Rosemary, Sage	To relieve headache
Checkerberry and Mint	Anti-Rheumatic

Susan R. Morton has suggested in *The Home Garden* magazine that the following four herbs be employed in summertime tisanes (served cold). The herbal quartet which are to provide the unique refreshments are: 1. Black Birch; 2. Hemlock; 3. Spice Bush; 4. New Jersey Tea. (Ed. Note: It is again suggested that an herb is to be drunk while still warm.)

Coffee Substitutes

Acorn Shells, Barley, Bedstraw, Chicory Root, Groundnut, Oats, Peanut Shells, Mexican (Chick) Pea, Rye, Soya Bean.

"Acorns," said a recent news report, "although just lately given official authorization in France, were favorably recommended in Europe more than one hunderd and fifty years ago. Father Tammany's *Almanac* for 1801, published by King & Baird, Philadelphia, described the findings of an eminent European physician on the value of acorns as a substitute for coffee, and the method of preparing it for consumption.

"The author states that acorns have always been esteemed as a wholesome, nourishing and strengthening nutriment for man, and by their medical qualities they have been found to remove nervous complaints when other medicines failed and that by roasting they lose their astringent quality."

One of the best, cheapest and most easily available coffee substitutes often grows in your own back yard or immediate environs. It is none other than Chicory (Wild Endive). I have found that ½ to 3 ounces of prepared Chicory added to 1 pound of coffee increases the yield by 30%, approximately 10 extra cups.

It requires no great effort to go to the corner market and purchase a 6 oz. box of ready-to-use Chicory for only 10 cents, and also the new available Chicory tablets, 40 for 10 cents, each tablet replacing one tablespoon of Coffee in preparing 5 to 6 cups. And since Chicory has long suffered the reputation of being used to adulterate ground coffee (usually by a small percentage of unscrupulous packers), most folks feel that the use of Chicory is undesirable, and after all, say they, "Who wants to bother digging up herb-roots and going to the trouble of roasting them, etc., etc.?"

But the method of preparing Chicory for use is quite simple. In mid-summer on a rainy day, after you have properly identified this herb, with its strong slender stem bearing the characteristic, now closed sky-blue flowers, dig up the roots and wash them clean, preferably with a brush. After slicing the roots in long thin strips, you are ready for either of two methods of preparing the roots for roasting. The first consists of tying together 5 or 6 of the strips with a thin wire, or leaving them untied, and allowing them to dry on, under or in an oven, in direct sunlight, or of course up in the dear old attic. The other method is to cut your sliced roots into thin transverse sections and then into quarters and allow them to dry. The roasting process for the quarter-sections is about the same as for the coffee bean. You may even place these smaller sections when dry inside a hot oven or directly on the washed-clean surface of your kitchen stove. The time limit is about 1 hour. However, the better method of roasting Chicory roots is to place several packages of the tied up root right in the midst of an outdoor fireplace. After a few minutes, the whites of the root centers will have turned a uniform brown; then these roots are to be ground, ready for use. The former method applies to the other coffee substitutes as Acorns, Cereals, Nuts and Peas and Soy Beans, except that no cutting is required.

When it comes to extending the family's coffee supply with any of these diluents, again remember that some sacrifice of flavor must be made, but by experiment and by using Chicory or Soy Bean or Peanuts, sparingly at first, you can suit the dilution to your own taste.

We may utilize friend Groundnut as a coffee diluent by scraping out the mealy interior and then roasting the balance which must be first cut into smaller segments. The more common cereals that have been used in past years to adulterate coffee—illegally of course—have been Rye, Barley and Oats, and I have no doubt but that these have-beens are now in the category of will-be's.

Since the Rye-Barley-Oats trio are rich in phosphate and iron, protein, and Vitamin A, B Complex and E, our future coffee compounds may soon be advertised as "a brand new discovery, a blend of coffee and nutritional vitamins," etc. One such food beverage that many today have found delicious is Zatzo, prepared by the Zatzo Food Corp. of Philadelphia, Pa. It is made of "Figs, Barley, Malt, Rye, Wholesome Nut and Roots of the Vegetable Kingdom."

Canning the Edible Herbs

The preservation of native fruits via jellies or jams has been proven to many housewives to be a profitable practice. The wild-growing fruits most commonly employed for this purpose are Rum and Choke Cherries, Barberries, Cranberries, Mulberries and Gooseberries. When making a jelly, it is best to add tart Apples to give it the needed jell-forming pectin that is not found in many fruits or berries. The fruits to be used in making a better jelly should be gathered preferably *before* they are thoroughly ripe and cooked per conventional recipes but in as little water as possible. Do use raw, unrefined sugar and not the white, refined sugar.

Profitable too will be found the practice of dehydration and the canning of surplus produce of one's vegetable garden and Nature's wildings, the edible herbs, which are plentiful, of very little cost and replete with health-fortifying nutrients.

Whatever reason is yours for canning, whether to "provide more vegetables for winter months". . . to "introduce vegetables and fruits to the non-eater of these vital foods". . . or "to preserve any surplus of farm produce, home grown and bought" (quoted from letters of listeners to "Your Health" broadcasts) it will be found, as one canning enthusiast wrote me, "Culinary herbs will greatly improve and break up the taste monotony of bland roots and vegetables, and help me to eat those foods which I do not particularly enjoy (?), but which I realize are good for me. . ." Or to quote Mrs. Grace Harrison, member of our Museum Herb Club, "You haven't lived until you've eaten my string bean preserves—enriched with Dill herb and Garlic, or with Basil." And Mrs. Fannie Smith, canning expert of the Club, has preserved most of the plentiful, health-fortifying products of Mother Nature's garden, which are listed below.

The art of cooking or preserving foods with herbs is an art of variety. Both the novice and experienced cook will truly marvel at the end results by the mere adding of a sprig or two of a given seasoning herb, thus accenting the "appetite appeal" of many vegetables (especially Beans and Burdock) and toning down the strongly flavored turnip.

Do not add herbs to the food while it is cooking. Always season by adding a sprig or a substantial pinch of herbs to each jar before bottling or capping.

Examples of edibles and their seasoning agents:

Wild Growing Edibles	*Culinary Herbs*
Barberries	Wild Allspice, Basil
Burdock	Wild Allspice, Basil
Wild (Skunk) Cabbage	Wild Onion
Cattail (young shoots)	Dill
Chickweed	Wild Garlic
Dandelion	Basil, Oregano
Lambsquarters	Basil
Marsh Marigold Buds	Dill, Wild Allspice
Milkweed	Dill
Nettle	Summer Savory
Pokeweed Shoots	Basil, Savory
Purslane	Basil, Savory
Sorrel	Garlic, Oregano

For further suggestions and the use and application of culinary herbs, read *Better Health with Culinary Herbs.*

Herbs and the Soil

There are many herbs that serve as excellent green manure or soil builders, and they are available at no monetary expense and can be easily obtained in one's leisure time. When our Museum Herb Club took over a deserted 100 x 100 ft. lot for vegetable cultivation, the soil was sandy and gravelly and hardly fit for the proper growth of Tomatoes, Potatoes and Corn; but since we were all organic-garden-minded, we were quite aware of the art of raising better produce without chemical and poisonous fertilizers and sprays. (However, we prepared our own herbal spray of Tobacco and Elder). Co-chairmen Stephen Ivanofski and Clovis Lefebre directed the operations while Marjorie Simpson led her specialized squad of "happy weeders" on daily tours collecting huge quantities of the required mineral-rich herbs which provided the nature-all fertilizer for the organic garden. We—the other members—gathered our contributions waiting for us along the roadsides, fields and brooksides, and from Clark University field we transported carloads of composted humus material to further enrich the hungry soil. Suffice it to say that following 15 months of intensive rebuilding of the soil, there was enough produce with which to supply the needs of the families of all our members and their cousins and their aunts.

Guided by our indefatigable co-chairmen, we carried on specific experiments which greatly helped us achieve far greater results than we had hoped for or expected. Not only did we compost any given excess that could not be utilized conveniently at a given time, for there were compost piles at 10 foot intervals along the perimeter and down through the rows; our freshly garnered herb greens were mulch-fed, as a salad, to the growing produce and then again stone-mulched. Stone mulching, it will be found, helps greatly to obviate the need of watering one's garden, small or large, during the hot rainless period.

The herbs best suited for this procedure are those that are found at arm's reach, Dandelion, Burdock, Lambsquarters, Pigweed and the Mustards, and these were also included in our Soil Activator. The ingredients of the Activator solution included the aforementioned plus 3 other equally important herbs, Sage, Nettle, and Chamomile. ("Chamomile produces a substance," writes Dr. Ehrenfried Pfeiffer, in *The Earth's Face and Human Destiny*, "which even in dilution of one to 125,000 millions, plainly stimulates yeast growth. . . . Growing here and there, [it] helps augment the yield of wheat.")

To prepare 5 gallons of the solution, a teaspoonful of dried ground horse or cow manure is placed in a gallon of water, preferably rain water, which is placed in the warm sun for 2 days. A cupful is carefully strained and added to a 5 gallon jar full of water to which is added a cupful of equal part of the herbs, dried and finely cut. This is allowed to stay in the warm sun for another 2 days and then the solution is sprayed or poured on to the recently turned or harrowed soil. At least twice a week in late Fall we performed this task, later spreading over the entire area a thick sheet of green manure, i.e. freshly collected green herbs, then our composted material and "imported" humus, and last of all, a thin spread of gravelly soil.

The non-smarting Smartweeds and Wild Buckwheats should also be used in soil building and serve even better than cultivated Buckwheat does. Dr. Saunders stated that since they make better growth on poor soil than Buckwheat, they will give more fertilizer to the soil than the latter. And he further avers: "Such weeds as these should be welcomed by the farmer and gardener. From the time the seeds sprout until the plants are in full bloom, they are capable of enrichening the soil they grow in if they are but plowed or hoed into it. He who fails to use these two troublesome weeds as soil builders has no appreciation of the need of decaying vegetable matter in soils."

Seaweed

This is a valuable manure for almost any description of soil, from the light sands to the heavy and viscid clays. No one who has experienced the beneficial results attending its application will doubt its value, especially when applied as a top-dressing to lands in grass. The most proper season for removing and spreading it, we are informed by those accustomed to its use, is immediately after haying, or if it cannot be conveniently done at this time, the work may be deferred till after harvest. It is a judicious plan to mix this weed with loam or muck, forming it into a sort of compost. The mass should be frequently turned. If convenient, ashes, lime, plaster and clay may be added, depending considerably upon what kind of soil the mass is to be applied to; but it should not be permitted to decay in a heap by itself, as in this case the limited amount of fibrous or ligneous substance contained in the mass causes it to decompose almost "to nothing"—a slight residuum only being left after decomposition, and this of a very weak character, and not, perhaps, of sufficient value to warrant its application to the soil.

When a farmer can obtain a sufficiency of this article with which to dress his lands, he need not fear the failure of his crops for lack of manure. Seaweed, and sea mud, or "flats," constitute an excellent substitute for animal excrement and compost, and almost supersede the necessity of the latter, in ordinary husbandry. If the weeds and mud should be taken out after haying, and placed in the barn or compost yard, with common muck, mold, and vegetable matters of a succulent and perishable character—or thrown into heaps with forest leaves, straw, weeds, etc., it would decompose, and by the next spring furnish an invigorating manure for every description of crop.

There is abundant testimony of the value of seaweed as a manure, in the books. Many years ago, the Highland Agricultural Society of Scotland charged an intelligent committee with the labor of investigating its composition and value, and their report is highly favorable. Dr. Holland, in his "Survey of Cheshire," says, "The ground thus manured not only gives a larger produce of potatoes, but is in a state of excellent preparation for a succeeding crop of either wheat or barley." In a work by the Rev. Philip Falle, upon the island of Jersey, whence we obtain the famous Jersey cattle, he says that "Nature having denied us the benefit of chalk, lime and marle, has supplied us with what fully answers the end of them in husbandry—it is a seaweed, but a weed more valuable to us than the choicest plant that grows in our garden. * * * Being spread thin on the green turf, and afterwards buried in furrows by the plow, it is incredible how, with its fat, unctuous substance, it ameliorates the ground, imbibing itself into it, softening the clod, and keeping the root of the corn moist during the most parching heats of summer."

We are aware that our friends on the seashore who have access to this plant value it highly. We suggest whether it has not sufficient value to justify its being collected away from our immediate shores, and landed up the creeks, and in such places as to bring it into the vicinity of a large extent of farming country.

"The weed flora," wrote Ehrenfried Pfeiffer, "is rich in information concerning the biological stability of the region and the changes going on within it. Even weeds have their task. They are a barometer for the soil's state of health. Since they have well-marked preferences for specific soil types and reactions, they immediately give the biologist information about the health or sickness of the landscape in question.

"Henbane and Stramonium, for example, are partial to limestone. The spreading Orach, *Atriplex patula*, is an indicator of the presence of humus, of manure fertilizing. It also associates with potatoes. . . . Soils tired out by grain culture and over-fertilized with lime and potassium show an increase of hedge mustard. Hedge mustard and Charlock like to grow in oat fields; they have a disturbing effect on the growth of rape and beets. Red clover, plantain and alfalfa like to grow in association. In old alfalfa-growing regions we see at blossoming time great patches yellow with dandelion. Among the most peculiar symbioses belongs the influence of garlic on roses, which heightens the production of the aromatic perfume substance in the rose. In this sphere can be included observations like those that caraway hinders the seed formation of fennel, coriander strengthens that of anise, wild pansies in a rye field have a markedly higher germination rate than elsewhere and much else of a similar nature."

The Herbs and Their Uses

"And the Fruit thereof shall be for meat, and the leaf thereof for medicine."—*Ezekiel* 47:12.

ACORN—*Quercus* Species*

Habitat: Sterile waste places.
Part Used: Nuts (fruits).
Collection: Early Fall.

Acorns have been eaten boiled and roasted,. and ground, have been made into bread. The roasted shells are a good coffee substitute. The Acorn meats have also been used as forage for hogs, cattle and domesticated animals.

Moreover, the Acorn is a much neglected source of

*Note: The Latinized names following most herbs are the scientific names or botanical origin, which, as arranged by the great Swedish botanist Linnaeus, Latinized for Karl von Linne, — and therefore the "(L.)"—serve to insure accuracy in botanical literature. He is often referred to as the father of modern botany for having been the first to establish the system of two names for plants. The first of the two names is the "genus" or generic name and corresponds to one's family name, Smith; and the second is the name of the species or specific name, which is analogous to one's given name, John.

The habitat of each herb is given to direct the attention of the herb collector to the proper locality or original home of the herbs. Thus, one should look for Skunk Cabbage and Marsh Marigolds in swamps, Peppergrass in gravelly soil and Purslane and Lambs-quarters in rich, garden soil.

When sugar is specified in the recipes, I mean the raw, brown and unrefined variety.

food and according to C. Hart Merriam, former chief of the U.S. Biological Survey, greater attention should be called to the highly nutritive values (as herein stated) of this widely distributed food.

It is important to remember that the constipating and dyspepsiating tannic acid, as of all native nuts, must first be removed by boiling the previously dried fruits (yes, nuts are the fruits of trees!) in a solution of lye obtained from wood-ashes, washing several times with cold water and removed and allowed to dry. White Oak Acorns contain much less tannic acid than other varieties, and need little lye treatment.

Contents: Calcium, Magnesium, Phosphorous, Potassium, Sulphur, Fat 37%, Protein 8%.

Ethnobotanist Huron H. Smith gives us a factual accounting of the Indians' method of converting Acorn meats into an edible flour in his *Ethnobotany of the Forest Potawatomi Indians*: "The forest Potawatomi use all kinds of Acorns indiscriminately for their starchy content, as a sort of breadstuff. In common with the other Indians of our region, they knew the secret of ridding the Acorns of their bitter tannic Acid. Hardwood ashes and water furnished the lye for soaking the Acorns which swelled them and removed the tannic Acid. A bark bag or reticule serves to hold the Acorns while they are washed through a series of hot and cold water to remove the lye. Then they are dried in the sun and become perfectly sweet and palatable. The Acorns were then dried for storage, and when wanted, pounded and ground to a coarse flour which was used to thicken soups or form a sort of mush. Blueberries were often cooked with this mush to give it a good flavor and it was seasoned with maple syrup.

"All the Ojibwe Indians tell of their former dependence upon the Acorn of the White Oak for their soup stock. It seems," says Smith, "that at least every Algon-

quin tribe knew and used all species of Acorns, getting
rid of the bitter tannin by soaking the Acorns in a hot
lye of wood ashes and boiling water.

"The Acorns were the real 'staff of life' and so important that Oaks which produced abundant crops were
considered, among most of the Pomo Indians of California, to be personal property. The ownership of these
trees was passed down in the family in accordance with
definite rules.

"The White Oak yielded the Indians their main
supply of Acorns," writes Dr. Smith, "which were used
for making soup, gruel, and mush, and also for making
both white and black bread (i.e. biscuits or cakes). The
black bread keeps very well. To help keep it moist, it is
sometimes put away in a wrapping of pendant moss.
Black bread is also sometimes purposely dried, especially by the aged. It becomes extremely hard and will then
keep indefinitely. When needed it can be readily softened by soaking in a little water a relatively short time.

"In the fall, when the Acorns are ripe, the Indians
gather them and spread them out to dry in the sun,
and when thoroughly dried, store them in large baskets
and wickerwork caches, sometimes in trees, but usually
on rocks or poles. These receptacles are built to shed
the rain and to keep out rats and mice, but are sufficient-
ly open to permit the circulation of air, thus avoiding
the danger of molding.

"Another and very different way of preserving
Acorns, practiced by the Wintoon Indians of western
Tehama County, in California, was described to me by
F.B. Washington, of Oakland. The Acorns were buried
in boggy places near cold springs, where they became
swollen and softened and turned nearly black in color,
but remained fresh for years. When needed they were
dug out and roasted, never dried or pounded for flour,
the mush and bread being always made of dried Acorns.

"White men in plowing have opened up caches of Acorns that had lain in these cold, boggy places for fully 30 years, and found the Acorns black, but still good.

"When preserved dry in the usual way, the Acorns are shucked as needed, and the dry meats, each splitting naturally in two parts, are pounded in stone mortars until reduced to a fine meal or flour. This at first is disagreeably bitter, but the bitter element is removed by leaching with warm water, which in seeping through acquires the color of coffee and the bitterness of quinine. The meal is then dried and stored to be used as required, for mush or bread.

"Mush and bread made wholly of acorn flour are not pleasing to our taste, but leached acorn meal mixed with corn meal in the proportion of one part acorn to four parts corn makes excellent corn bread and pones, and mixed with white flour or whole-wheat flour in the same proportion makes palatable bread and muffins, adding to the cereal value the value of a fat nut product.

"I have often eaten the pure acorn mush and bread as made by the Indians, but prefer the mixed product above mentioned. John Muir, during his arduous tramps in the mountains of California, often carried the hard, dry acorn bread of the Indians and deemed it the most compact and strength-giving food he had ever used."

Another kind of bread was made by the Indians of Sacramento Valley. The eminent geologist, James D. Dana, who traversed the valley with the Wilkes Expedition in 1841 said: "Throughout the Sacramento plains the Indians live mostly on a kind of bread or cake made of acorns . . . kneaded into a loaf about two inches thick, and baked. It has a black color, and a consistency like that of cheese, but a little softer; the taste, though not very pleasing, is not positively disagreeable."

"Acorn bread is black as jet, and while still fresh
has the consistency of rather soft cheese. In the course
of a few days it becomes hard. It is remarkable for being
sweet, for the original meal, and even the soup, are
rather insipid. The sweet taste is very evident, and is
due in great measure to the prolonged and gentle cooking, which, favored by the moisture of the dough, grad-
ually converts some constituent of the meal into sugar."

Indians Establish Acorn Camps in Autumn

"A very intelligent full-blood woman named Che-
na-wah Weitch-ah-wah, belonging to the Po-lik-lah or
lower Klamath tribe," wrote C. Hart Merriam a half-
century ago in the *National Geographic Magazine*, "says
that in her country when the acorns ripen, in late October
and November, the families establish acorn camps in
favorite localities, gathering and bringing in the nuts in
the large burden baskets. In the evening, when the evening meal is finished, all the family—men, women, and
the children—engage in removing the hulls with their
teeth, an occupation at which they are very expert. The
hulled green acorns are put into large, flattish circular
receptacles of basket work, which are placed on top of a
high frame over the fire in the house, so that the heat in
rising dries them. . . .

"It is known that Algonkin tribes of our Eastern States used acorns for bread and for oil, and mixed
boiled acorns with their fish and meat.

"The Iroquois of the state of New York, according
to F. W. Waugh, commonly made use of acorns for food,
apparently favoring the sweet kinds, as those of the white
and chestnut oaks. . .

"Waugh states further that nut meats (presumably
including acorns) were pounded, boiled slowly in water,
and the oil skimmed off into a bowl; the oil was boiled
again and seasoned with salt, to be used with bread,
potatoes, pumpkins, squashes, and other foods, and nut

oil was often added to mush. The meats left after skimming off the oil were seasoned and mixed with mashed potatoes, and nut meats were crushed and added to hominy and corn soup to make it rich.

"There is every reason to believe that a fair proportion of the species might be utilized with advantage to vary or supplement the daily diet of the people. This would be especially desirable in the case of the ill-nourished poorer classes—those subject to the inroads of hookworm and pellagra."

Acorns as a Bread Substitute in Europe

In the same article Merriam continued, "In England, France, and Italy, during periods of food scarcity boiled acorns were used as a substitute for bread; and in most of the Mediterranean countries the sweet fruit of *Quercus esculenta* (mind the name) is still prized by the inhabitants. In Algeria and Morocco the large acorns of an evergreen oak are eaten both raw and roasted, while in Spain those of the Gramont oak are regarded as even superior to chestnuts.

"V. K. Chestnut quotes Giovanni Memmo to the effect that in Spain and Italy sometimes as much as 20 per cent of the total food of the poorer people consists of sweet acorns. But as the indigestible tannin is not removed, it has been found that 10 per cent of the acorns pass away undigested. The superiority of the methods employed by our Indians is obvious.

"That a food of such genuine worth should be disregarded by our people is one of many illustrations of the reluctance of the white man to avail himself of sources of subsistence long utilized by the aborigines."

Twelve Different Acorns

"To the average person an acorn is just an acorn and nothing more," says a story in *Horticulture*. "The botanist, however, and other persons familiar with trees know that acorns appear in at least 12 different forms, representing as many different oak species. Most persons probably have seen only a few kinds and do not realize the wide variation which exists. Most boys brought up in the country gather and eat acorns every season, but in parts of Europe, and perhaps elsewhere, acorns are used as a part of a regular diet. It is well known, of course, that swine feed on them eagerly but observers have found that they are also eaten by deer and by some wild birds. The oak itself is a very old tree —so old in fact that it was mentioned frequently in ancient mythology. Moreover, it is a tree which is able to endure the rigors of exposed positions and the attacks of insect pests."

Comparative Analyses of Corn Meal, Wheat Flour, and Acorn Flour

| | Corn Meal | Wheat Flour | Acorn Flour | |
			Leached	Unleached
Water	12.5	11.5	11.34	5.82
Ash	1.0	.5	.29	1.90
Fat	1.9	1.0	19.81	25.31
Protein	9.2	11.4	4.48	5.44
Carbohydrates	74.4	75.4	62.02	59.62
Fiber	1.0	.2	2.06	1.91

U.S. Food Administration

BLACK ALDER *Ilex Verticillata*

The leaves of this decorative swamp dweller are collected in the Summer, dried and used as a tea-substitute.

Beware the red berries: Eaten in the fresh state, they are highly cathartic and such eating may also cause nausea and vomiting.

ALFALFA—*Medicago Sativa* (*L.*)

Synonym: Buffalo Herb, Sweet Lucerne.
Part Used: Young tender leaves, flowering tops.

Collection: Spring to early Summer.

Preparation: Eat uncooked. Add to vegetable salad, cole slaw, or prepared cereal (cooked oatmeal).

Tisane: To prepare a health tea or Pekoe tea substitute, use equal parts of Alfalfa and Spearmint leaves. Drink a warm tea 4 or 5 times a day.

No doubt, many have seen Alfalfa growing in nearby farmlands serving as a soil enricher and along the country roadsides, though few have realized that the leaves are as, if not more, wholesome than any of the usual store-bought cereals.

Alfalfa is an excellent source of quickly assimilated vitamins and minerals. True, it is fed to cattle and horses, but today many convalescents are drinking the above mentioned Alfalfa-Spearmint teas, infants are being fed Pablum, a cereal which contains powdered leaf Alfalfa, and, too, there are Alfalfa tablets.

Sometime in May or June, collect several bunches of the herb at some neighborly farmer's land and after drying them by suspension in the rear hall or attic, strip the leaves from the stems and grind them up as finely as desired. The next time that a hot or cold cereal is to be served, serve yourself a new treat with a liberal sprinkle of ground Alfalfa leaves.

We found it fun experimenting, or let us say pioneering, in utilizing this highly nutritious foodstuff. I had claimed in my radio broadcasts as early as 1939 that Alfalfa (as well as green Grass, Watercress, et al) would soon appear on the market under the assorted high priced trade names. Now many "Nature Food" and health stores throughout the country stock Alfalfa tablets, plain or compounded with other dehydrated vegetables, Parsley, Watercress, etc., as a food supplement.

True, it takes real pioneer spirit to undertake for the first few times the eating of ground Alfalfa leaves

as a cereal substitute, which no doubt will sooner or
later appear on market shelves under the usually varied,
competitive tradenames. However, by virtue of its roots'
deep-soil penetration, and therefore the excellent extraction of the priceless ingredients of the Good Earth,
Alfalfa will provide in a quick, assimilable manner 14 of
the 16 principal mineral elements and all the now known
vitamins.

"There is about $800 worth of vitamins (if you
bought them in pill form) in just one acre of alfalfa," says
Herbert M. Barnes of Ohio State University.

Alfalfa Aids Jaundice Cure

A busy doctor friend of mine drove his automobile up beside
mine in the parking place at the hospital the other day. Looming
out of the back was a stack of green grass and clover. "What in
the world is that load you are hauling?" I asked.

"Alfalfa," he answered. "A dose or two for a patient of mine.
Didn't you know that Alfalfa is the very newest treatment?"

I did know it because Alfalfa is supposed to be the best source
of the new vitamin—vitamin K.

A story I heard goes as follows:

A woman was brought into this famous American hospital with
jaundice. The jaundice had come on suddenly and deepened rapidly
in 3 or 4 days. Up to the time of the onset she was perfectly well.
She became, as the saying goes, "as yellow as a pumpkin."

Then she began to bleed from her nose, from the bowel, and
clots of blood formed spontaneously under her skin.

It is well known that bile in the blood—which is what jaundice
is—is liable to prevent the clotting of blood. Surgeons are very
loath to do a surgical operation on a patient with jaundice for that
reason. It was evident that this woman had some impediment to the
clotting from the nose, under the skin, etc. It was found by the
laboratory test that the prothrombin in her blood was only 5 percent
of what it ought to be. Prothrombin is an element in the blood which
is necessary for clotting.

Finally a new consultant was called in who said that he had
heard of a disease of cattle, due to eating spoiled clover, and that it
was cured by feeding alfalfa.—*News Report*

"The time will come," predicted Irene Wheeler
in *New Physical Culture*, "when Alfalfa will be recog-

nized as an important source of human blood food. Its roots, growing to a depth of twenty to fifty feet, extract values from the earth that no other plant can reach.

"A tea made of Alfalfa (leaves and stems) is most nourishing and delicious—served with or without milk and sweetened with honey—or mixed with juices, soups, etc. Especially fine for children or rundown people. Cell building, alkaline and mildly laxative, there are many ways to use Alfalfa and all to great advantage in promoting health".

Get Vitamins A and D From Alfalfa

G.B. Lal, writing in Meyer's *Almanac*, reported the "discovery of a new process for increasing the supply of Vitamins A and D, and other food substances essential for normal health and morale of the nation.

"The notable feature of the new process is that it makes it possible to produce these food factors for man out of green plants like Alfalfa.

"Vitamins A and D, as available hitherto, are derived from fish liver oils, and have fishy taste and odor. The same vitamins prepared from Alfalfa leaf-meal appear to be free of any taste and odor.

"Actually, the material obtained by the new method is 'pro-vitamin A,' that is, a substitute which is turned into Vitamin A within the human body, provided there is enough fat in the diet. Treatment of this pro-vitamin with ultra-violet rays produdes Vitamin D."

* * *

Ever since Alfalfa has been considered "cow-food," herb-users and herbalists have recommended this plant to those afflicted with peptic ulcers or jaundice. "Don't know what's in that Alfalfy," old timers would say, "but you take it morning, noon, and twice at night and you'll be good as new in a few months."

Some years ago, it was reported that the oil obtained from Alfalfa leaf was a chief source of Vitamin K, which even in the experimental stage had proven its effectiveness in stopping severe hemorrhages following gall-bladder operations. Alfalfa proved to be a new cheap commercial source of Vitamins A and D, thus replacing fish oils which had become scarce due to wartime fishing restrictions. Alfalfa leaf is an ingredient of the popular predigested cereal, Pablum.

Medicinally, Alfalfa has been used as an anti-hemorrhagic in peptic ulcers, due to its Vitamin K contents, where low prothrombin is indicated. (Vitamin K exists also in Spinach and Tomatoes.) The herb has been much used by lay and professional herbalists in combination with Red Clover and with either Spearmint or Peppermint, which combination also provides one with an excellent Pekoe tea substitute.

WILD ALLSPICE—*Lindera Benzoin* (L.)

Part Used: Leaves, fruits, ground young twigs.
Collection: The leaves and young twigs are gathered in Summer, and the ripe berries in Autumn, and all are to be carefully dried by suspension.

This is an early blooming shrub and is found along banks of brooks and in swampy woods. As a member of the Laurel family this aromatic shrub claims relationship to the better known Sassafras, Camphor and Cinnamon, the better to remind the enterprising kitcheneer of its flavoring possibilities. A true herald of Springtime and its pleasantries, the herb proclaims the initial joys of the season by showing off its clusters of small yellow flowers. In early Autumn we find the bunches of the oval, bright red berries on stout, short stalks.

Since all the parts of this shrub yield an aromatic oil, its true fragrance is far better evaluated when it is used instead of the original harsh Allspice, as it was by many New England housewives in the early 1800's. When pickling Cucumbers or preserving Beets, season

with your home-made native Herb Vinegar which includes the twigs and fruits of this herb.

A new taste in a tisane is afforded by mixing equal
portions of its finely ground, dried leaves, and any Mint
and Orange peel. During the War of Independence, the
fruits were substituted for Allspice, and its leaves brewed as an after-dinner drink instead of the imported
Chinese tea. Thus, its synonyms Wild Allspice and
Spice Bush.

AMARANTH—*Amaranthus Blitum* (L.)

Synonym: Pigweed, Strawberry Blite.
Part Used: Young leaves, seeds.
Collection: Throughout Spring and Summer when
shoots are 6-8 inches high.
Preparation: Uncooked in salads. Cooked as pot herb
spinach.

When young, Amaranth should be considered a
vitamin-packed companion to Carrot and Beet and is
best eaten uncooked as a salad green. It should also be
considered a good pot herb and Spinach substitute
served either with butter or with oil and vinegar. Since
Lambsquarters and Amaranth are indicators of healthy,
organically cultured gardens, one should take advantage
of their profuse growth, dry their edible portions and
keep storing them throughout the summer so that during
winter one may have ample vegetable material for soup
or a steamed salad plate. To provide additional food
source, the Indians also used the shiny black Amaranth
seeds which were sometimes first parched and then
ground into meal and either baked into cakes or included in porridge.

ANGELICA—*Angelica Atropurpurea* (L.)

Parts Used: Leaves, stems, roots and seeds.
Collection: The leaves in Spring, and the stems in Summer, up to mid-July; the seeds, before ripening; the

roots of the first year's growth in September. Since
the roots are fleshy and very apt to be attacked by
insects and mold, they should be dried quickly and
conserved in air-tight jars, with the added protection
of a few drops of carbon tetrachloride or carbon di-
sulphide. The roots, so protected, will stay in good
condition for 2 to 3 years. And be careful in tasting
the juice of the fresh root since, as in the case of
Jack-in-the-Pulpit, it is somewhat acrid and may
cause a temporary burning sensation. Upon drying,
however, the root loses this acridity.

Note: Any excess of leaves should be washed and dried,
ground and preserved in mason jars, thus providing an extra source of nourishment during the winter months when soup greens are scarce.

There is an old belief among the Laplanders who
claim that Angelica strengthens life and, therefore, chew
it as some here do tobacco. Dr. William Woodville in
his *Medical Botany* (1810), reports the findings of Linnaeus regarding its popularity amongst the Laplanders:
"They entertain a high opinion of the utility of Angelica
and employ it both as food and as a medicine; and since
aromatic plants are rarely inhabitants of the Polar regions, their partiality for Angelica is extremely natural."
As a medicine these people use the herb as a stomachic,
sudorific and carminative.

In Europe the root and stem are candied and eaten
as a conserve. Angelica root has been used as an aromatic
in flatulence, colic and also as a domestic diaphoretic and
diuretic, and occasionally externally as a counterirritant.
The seeds were at one time supposed to possess antima-
larial properties.

The fresh or dried, diced leaves may be included
in stews and soups but should be added during the last
few minutes of cooking. Use a half tablespoonful of the
dried leaves (or one of the fresh leaves) to a pot, for a
serving of four.

The stems may be blanched, or cut in 6-inch lengths and prepared as Asparagus. Cut into 1-inch segments, they can be added to soups with the other ingredients.

The candied roots are a worthy substitute for the prepared Ginger and Sweet Flag, and in this capacity as a gentle carminative and stomachic, especially suitable for the elderly.

Candied Angelica

1. Cut the (young) roots into lengths, cover with just enough water, and boil until tender, 15 to 20 minutes. Peel and boil again until green.

2. Dry the roots and to every ounce, add an ounce of sugar.

3. Let stand two days and boil gently the ingredients again until clear (or until the syrup begins to crystallize).

4. Remove the roots, strew powdered sugar over them and allow to dry thoroughly on wax paper. Store in small air-tight glass jars.

Note: Save the syrup, which affords one with a simple remedy possessing the therapeutic benefits of herb Angelica: Carminative, Stomachic and Expectorant. The dose is a teaspoonful mixed in a little warm water sipped slowly as often as required.

As stated above, the aromatic stems are to be added as seasoning. The inch lengths of the root and seeds help to savorize a fish or meat stew and fresh vegetable or bean soup. To each potful, limit the root to 2 inch lengths, which are removed before serving, and about ½ teaspoonful of the seeds. Try a sprig of the fresh leaves or a short leaf stalk as seasoning for fish, baked or broiled.

Old Tamarack's Tobacco Habit Remedy, #712

"Take about a teaspoonful of Angelica ('Archangel') Root ground fine, and place it in your cheek, but swallow the juice. This is a good substitute for tobacco, and an excellent tonic for the stomach, and also for some nervous troubles, especially such as are due to using tobacco." This recipe is from Meyer's *Herbalist*.

ARROWHEAD—*Sagittaria. Latifolia* (L.)

Synonym: Tule Potato, Wapatoo.
Part Used: Corms (tubers).
Collection: The corms which develop upon the short rootlets may break away from the root mass very easily, so care must be taken in digging them "in situ." Attached to the roots are the runners which held the globular tubers, about one inch or the size of a small walnut. Any surplus may be dried by suspension and used later when needed.

The tubular roots were collected by the Chippewa Indians in the Fall, strung and hung overhead in the wigwam to dry. Later when needed for use, they were cooked or boiled and eaten as a Potato substitute. The Ojibwe prepared and used the tubers in similar fashion, cooking and serving them with deer meat and Maple syrup. We are told that some of these Arrowhead Potatoes are kept over even after cooking and the Maple syrup is thickened "until they might almost be called candied sweet Potatoes."

The roundish corms are pure-white inside and of a sweetish starchy texture and may be substituted for and prepared like the Potato, baked or boiled. Moreover, we have found the tubers even more tasty when roasted in the wood-ashes of an open air oven or fireplace. Eat them sliced or mashed with butter or cheese. Arrowhead corms are easily ground fine, yielding a flour with which one may prepare spice cookies, muffins and fruit puddings.

Lewis and Clark record how at the Willamette River (which joins the Columbia) the native tribes subsisted chiefly on Wapatoo or Arrowhead. Each tuber was the size of a hen's egg and closely resembled the Potato. It was their chief vegetable to eat with fish or meat and an important article of trade and never out of season. When they reached the mouth of the Columbia, their journals reveal, "We purchased, from the old squaw, for armband and rings, a few Wapatoo roots on which we subsisted. They are nearly equal in flavor to the Irish Potato and afford a very good substitute for bread."

JERUSALEM ARTICHOKE— *Helianthus Tuberosus* (L.)

Habitat: Banks of brooks, wet places.

Part Used: The tubers (roots).

Collection: In late Fall. The tubers should be left covered in sandy soil until needed.

Preparation: Artichokes are used as an article of nutritious food, especially as a Potato substitute. For table use, they may be boiled or baked preferably, pureed with peas and similar vegetables or included in soups or stews. The smaller crisp tubers are often pickled or made into relish.

Mrs. C. F. Leyel, in her *Elixir of Life*, wrote that when the roots were first introduced into England, they were called Potatoes of Canada, and were sometimes stewed with wine and spices and sometimes baked in pies.

One writer states that the tubers "may be used in every way as the Potato; and are suited to persons in delicate health when debarred from the use of most other vegetables."

The tubers contain a principle analogous to starch (inulin), and a large proportion of uncrystallized sugar.

This plant is not a native of Jerusalem or of the Near East, as the name implies. "Jerusalem" is a corruption of the Italian *girasole*. It is one of the oldest cultivated vegetables and was known to the Greeks and Romans.

Without doubt, averred Prof. Oliver Medsger, it

was the Jerusalem Artichoke that Captains Lewis and
Clark described in their journal under date of April 9,
1805, when, in what is now North Dakota, "we stopped
for dinner, the squaw Sacajawea went out and after
penetrating with a large stick the holes of mice [probably
prairie dogs or gophers] near some driftwood, brought
to us a quantity of wild Artichokes, which the mice collect and hoard in large numbers. . . Its flavor as well
as the stalk which issues from it resembles those of the
Jerusalem Artichoke, except that the latter is much
larger."

   (*See*: *Growing the Jerusalem Artichoke*, Leaflet No. 116,
1959, United States Dept. of Agriculture.)

Allied Plant: The Showy Sunflower, *Helianthus Lati-
   florus*, produces tubers that are said to be a little in-
   ferior to those of the cultivated Artichoke.

FLOWERING ASH—*Chionanthus Virginica* (L.)

Synonym: Fringe Tree.
Habitat: Native to lower New England, along the edges
   of streams.
Part Used: The fruits.
Collection: Midsummer.
Preparation: The fruits may be preserved in cider or
   herb vinegar and served as a pickle for table use.

BAMBOO BRIER—*Smilax Caduca* (L.)

Synonym: Green-, Cat-, House Brier.
Habitat: Open woods, thickets.
Part Used: Young shoots, 5-6 inches, the tender leaves.
Collection: Spring and early Summer.
Preparation: Brier shoots and leaves are used in soups
   or prepared as a cooked vegetable. Whenever possible, the leaves should be eaten uncooked or,
   flavored mildly with an herb vinegar, mixed into
   a vegetable salad or finely cut into cole slaw.

BARBERRY—*Berberis Vulgaris* (L.)

Synonym: Sourberry.
Habitat: Drywoods. Garden hedge.
Part Used: Berries.
Collection: Late Fall.
Preparation: The red football-shaped fruits are sour and
    tart and contain pectin, thus providing an excel-
    lent source with which to prepare a native jam,
    jelly or preserve. The berries may well replace
    Cranberries to prepare a tart sauce or pies.

With Lemon and Mint, they are used as a cooling
Summer drink and as a general thirst-quencher.

Several centuries ago, the Egyptians made good use
of a diluted juice of the berries in "ardent and pestilential
fever," jaundice, "fluxes," etc. . . . Their method of
preparation, to which is accorded "the most happy success," was to infuse the berries for one full day (24
hours) in ten times their weight of warm water, then
straining and sweetening the liquid with sugar or a
syrup of Lemon or Orange.

An excess of berries should be dried and later used
medicinally or as indicated above.

May I ask you, what are you going to do with that
basketful of Barberry bush cuttings, chuck full of those
red berries? Discard the cuttings as you see fit, but be
sure to save the berries. Not only did our Massachusetts
Indians use the roots of this shrub as a stimulating tonic
for cases of liver complaints but they ate these "sour
berries," as they called these red fruits, in the form of a
tart jelly or jam. And now, in October, you can do the
same according to your culinary taste and desires; you
may prepare with barberries an excellent sauce, in manner similar to cranberries.

The following 19th century recipe comes from the
New England Farmer:

"Barberry jelly, ruby clear, is the finest table jelly to serve with venison and other high-flavored roasts, and epicures will have no other when they have once tried it. Heat the berries in a close-covered stone jar, without water, till the juice flows; put them in a bag of double cheese-cloth tied tight, and press them on a slanting pastry board or marble slab, with a rolling pin. The juice runs into a dish below. Add white [*Ed.* No, brown!] sugar, measure for measure, and boil with very gentle heat, covering close. The barberry comes too late in the year to make jelly by sunshine. Set the stone jar of juice and sugar in the oven, or in a kettle of boiling water, and let it take its time. I have kept my jellies open for weeks, and they suffered no harm.

"Every thoroughbred house keeper will put up barberry syrup when she learns its value for invalids' use. As a medicine for consumptives, it has more than the virtue ascribed to lemons, and barberries, lemons and grapes are a trinity of restoratives for which too much can hardly be said.

"Pick two quarts of berries from the stems, and boil in one quart of filtered water till they are soft; strain through flannel, and for every pint, add a pint and a half of sugar. Boil quite thick, as for table syrup, and when cold, bottle and seal, keeping in a cold, dry place. Let invalids drink this diluted with cold water as often and as freely as they can relish it."

Here are three more 19th century recipes from W. A. Henderson's *Modern Domestic Cookery*.

1. *Barberry Wine*

"Express enough of the fruits to yield a quart of juice, to which add 3 quarts of water and 3 pounds of sugar and allow the mixture to ferment: or, 2 quarts of hot water down to 2 quarts and continue as described. This makes a pleasant drink when mixed with 3 or 4 times the amount of water."

2. *Pickled Barberries*

"Dissolve a half pound sugar in a quart of Cider vinegar, add a pint of the fruits and a sufficient amount of seasoning, and boil until a good color appears. Allow to stay covered until cold. Strain and bottle. The fruits and resultant liquor are suitable for a tart sauce, relish or spread."

3. *Preserved Barberries*

"To preserve Barberries for tarts, you must proceed thus: Pick the fruits, take their weight of loaf sugar and put them in a jar. Set them in a kettle of boiling water till the sugar is melted, and then let them stand all night. The next day, put them into a preserving pan and boil them 15 minutes, then put them into jars, tie them closely, and set them by for use."

BARNYARD GRASS—*Echinochloa Crusgalli*

Synonym: Cockspur Grass, Hedgehog Grass.

Habitat: Rich, cultivated soil.

Part Used: The ripe seeds.

Collection: Mid-Summer to Fall.

Preparation: Cut off the entire clusters of seeds; place them in paper bags and dry them by spreading out the seed heads on cardboard, preferably in the attic. The seeds may be cooked in soups and stews or with Peas and baked Beans.

BEDSTRAW—*Galium Aparine* (L.)

Synonym: Goosegrass, Cleavers.

Habitat: Moist thickets.

Part Used: Early sprouts. Seeds.

Collection: Spring to early Summer.

Preparation: The young sprouts may be steamed a minute or two and mixed with other vegetables; they may be served uncooked with similar "salad" herbs like Sorrel and Chickweed.

During the past few centuries, it has been recommended as a "reducing" herb. Dr. John Gerard in his *Herball* (1597) had urged all buxom women to "make pottage of cleavers with a little mutton and oatmeal, to cause lanknesse and keepe them from fatnesse." Herbalist John Parkinson also had advised that the herb be "taken in broth to keepe them leane and lanke that are apt to grow fat." Bedstraw was once considered a "blood purifier" and was therefore a common ingredient in spring broth.

The seeds of Bedstraw offer a very good substitute for coffee, revealing the fact that Bedstraw and Coffee are members of the same family. The roasted seeds of the former once dried and slightly roasted, yield an aroma much like that of coffee.

The synonym Goosegrass refers to the fact that geese and other poultry, as well as horses and cows, do eat this herb and appear not to be affected by its "reducing" qualities.

YELLOW BEDSTRAW, *Galium Verum*

The flowers and herb are said to be employed to curdle milk, for the preparation of cheese. Both Dioscorides and Galen attribute to it this quality and Mathiolus informs us that the early Tuscans used it for this purpose, in order that the cheese they made from the milk of sheep and goats "may eat [taste] the sweeter."

Herbalist Gerard stated that the people of Namptwich use the herb in their rennet, "esteeming it to be the best cheese that is made with it, and in some of the Western Isles, they curdle milk with a strong decoction of this herb."

BEECHNUTS— *Fagus Grandifolia* (L.)—(*Fagus Sylvatica*—European Beech)

A most lovely, large and lofty tree, the Beech is found in rich soil and is of great economic importance, as a source of food. Its generic name, *Fagus*, is derived from a Greek word meaning "to eat," "either because mankind," Thomas Green explains, "lived on Beechnuts before the use of corn, or because it was the food of the common people."

The Beech twin nuts are collected in late Fall and yield sweet and edible kernels. They have been used extensively as feed for poultry and farm animals in England and France, where Beechnut oil is much used instead of butter. European farmers give them to their hogs to fatten them for market. The highly nutritious nuts are small, about ½ inch long, but very sweet. Dried and powdered, the nutmeal is made into wholesome bread.

The Acorn method is used in preparing them for food. The nuts may be roasted to provide a coffee substitute.

Contents: Calcium, Chlorine, Magnesium, Phosphorus, Potassium, Silicon and Sulphur. Fat—42%, Protein—22%.

Beechnuts are best eaten with uncooked vegetables.

Note: At the beginning of the 18th century, Aaron Hill had a project for paying off England's national debt with the oil of Beechnut, but they seemed to yield so little oil in the northern country that, Linnaeus informs us, scarcely any oil could be expressed from them.

RED BERGAMOT—*Monarda Didyma* (L.)

Part Used: The upper half of the herb.

The Boston Tea Party will long be remembered as the result of the rising protest against the despised taxes on imported tea. In their boycott against the use of the imported beverage item, the patriots accepted three out of a number of native substitutes for the China tea. Choice number one was then known as Oswego, and

later as Bee Balm, synonym for this handsome perennial. The other two were Labrador Tea, *Ledum palustre*,
which was favored by the patriots of the more northern
states, and New Jersey Tea, *Ceanothus americanus*, by
those of the southern area. Any of these 3 offers a real
health drink since none contains caffeine nor any other
harmful principle.

Whoever wishes to drink a tea of "pleasing" herbs
instead of heart-stimulating Pekoe tea will find in *Monarda* an invaluable ally who has earned a well-deserved
niche in tisanology. Its healthful refreshment and delectable fragrance give further evidence of such a preference,
as does its down-to-earth aesthetic value in the flower
garden. Variety in a tisane of *Monarda* is obtained by
adding culinaries Sage or Basil or freshly ground, dried
peels of Orange or Lemon, or a combination of these
four.

Its name and synonyms help to better establish its
historical significance. It is called Oswego Tea because
the herbalists and Shakers who settled in that area
found the herb growing in wild profusion in the environs of Oswego, N. Y., and soon began to pluck the
leaves of this two-plus-footer for their tisanes. And, too,
they may well have learned of its employment from the
native Oswego Indians. It is interesting to note that the
English owe their knowledge of this charming plant to
an American, a Mr. J. Bartram of Philadelphia, who, as
far back as 1744, sent seeds to a friend in England where
it flowered the following year. Mr. Bartram had found
the plant growing at Oswego, N.Y. The name Bee Balm
obviously signifies the attention given by the bees to the
nectar of this herb. (Balm, per se, generally refers to
Lemon Balm). The generic name, *Monarda*, serves to
remind us that the herb was named after the famous
16th century Spanish physician, Nicholas Monardez.

One or two of the smaller sized leaves, freshly

picked and washed, may be added whole to a fruit cup and cut for a mixed nut and fruit jelly mold. A jelly, prepared with infusion of the larger leaves, dried, is a suitable companion for poultry and fish dishes.

Associated Plants: 1. Wild Bergamot, *Monarda fistula*, is generally found growing along roadside or sandy areas.

2. Horsemint (Syn. Water Pennyroyal), *Monarda punctata* (L.), is an important medicinal herb whose leaves and flowering tops are collected when in full bloom. It is a suitable substitute for Mint or Catnip or other mild aromatics. Its excellent carminative and calmative properties provide in this plant a most useful remedy in flatulence and nervous colic. Its diaphoretic property is accentuated if taken in hourly doses.

Unassociated Plants: (True) Bergamot, *Citrus aurantium* (L.) variety *Bergamia*. This is a small tree and its leaves yield the essential oil which is employed in the manufacture of Eau de Cologne and various perfumes.

BIRCH (SWEET)—*Betula Lenta* (L.)

Synonym: Black Birch, Cherry Birch.
Habitat: Woods, hillsides.
Collection: Midsummer.
Preparation: The ground leaves and twigs may be added to the list of ingredients which enter the "native herb vinegar" recipe. Finely ground, they may be used to flavor soups.

A mixture of equal parts of the ground leaves and twigs and Peppermint, Savory and Bee Balm is well adapted as a tea or coffee substitute, or as a refreshing tisane taken between meals. To prepare the herb tea: Steep a teaspoonful of the herbs in a cup of hot water, cover and allow to cool. Stir, strain, and drink one such cupful as desired, or four times a day.

Wish a good source of the much-needed trace elements of minerals in organic form and all freshly provided for you from the soil? Gather your own leaves of the common Birches, prepare them as a tisane, as above, and this store of minerals is yours: Calcium, chlorine, copper, iron, magnesium, phosphorus, potassium, sodium and silicon. And in addition the herb will present you with a gift of vitamins "not synthetically made by man but organically and biologically made by Nature's own processes of life"— Carotene or Vitamins A, C, E and two of the Vitamin B family, B_1 and B_2.

I have found it recorded that "in 1861 after the battle of Carrick's Ford, the edible bark of Black Birch probably saved the lives of hundreds of Garnett's Confederate soldiers during their retreat to Monterey, Va. For a number of years after that, the route the soldiers took could be traced by the peeled Birch trees.

"The Black Birch and Yellow Birch are also noted for their abundant sap. The former is sometimes tapped for the purpose of making a sort of beer from the fermented sap."

A beer or wine has been prepared from the saccharine juice that flows out from the stem of the tree, when wounded. The juice is also used to make an herb vinegar.

Birch Sap

"The River Birch (*Betula Nigra*) is, indeed, a river of refreshment in March when the sap is running and refuses no thirsty wayfarer who taps it," says a writer in the *Philadelphia Record*.

"Thrust your knife into the bark," directed O. W. Barrett in the *American Botanist*, "insert a splinter at a declining angle, hold a cup to catch the drippings and you have in a few minutes a mouthful of a beverage as clear and cool as spring water, with the faintest possible suggestion of sugar in it.

"When it is boiled down, it requires only a few

quarts of the fresh sap to make a generous dish of a highly flavored reddish waxy sugar. As a boy on the old Vermont farm, I used to delight to drink the clear, cool, aromatic sap of an old black Birch which stood out among the Maples and was tapped in the usual manner—partly for fun and partly for the delicious and healthful beverage it afforded."

Birch Wine

Here is another recipe from Henderson's *Modern Domestic Cookery.*

"This wine must be made at that time of the year when the liquor from the Birch tree can best be procured. That is, in the beginning of March, when the sap is rising and before the leaves shoot out. . . . Take the sap and boil it as long as any scum will rise, skimming it all the time. To every gallon of liquor use 4 pounds of good sugar and the thin peel of a Lemon. Then boil it half an hour and keep skimming it well. Pour it into a clean tub and when it is almost cold, set it to work with yeast spread upon a toast. Let it stand 5-6 days, stirring often. Then take a cask just large enough to hold all the liquor. . . turn your wine, and lay the bung on lightly till you find it has done working. Stop it, close and after 3 months bottle it off."

BLACKBERRY—*Rubus* Species

Synonym: Bramble Bush.
Habitat: Roadsides, waste places.
Part Used: The fruits.
Collection: Mid-Summer, when ripe.

To better enjoy the wholesome richness of these fruits one must not be too eager to pick them. They must be soft to the touch—yes, vine-ripened and sweet to the taste. On herb-collecting tours, my four sons had learned to recognize the best time for gathering: "They're

ripe! The bees are on the berries and telling us to pick
them now!"

As the fruits ripen, they lose their astringency, i.e.
the tannic acid content is safely lodged in the root, for
which reason the unripe berries and root have been used
since Biblical days as an astringent for dysentery, and as
a gargle.

Often during the Civil War, truces were declared
so that soldiers might forage for wild Blackberries. They
were recognized as a preventive of dysentery, summer
complaints, and other digestive disturbances.

However, the ripe sweet fruits are to be used as are
other sub-acid fruits, Raspberries, Elderberries, etc. Although best eaten uncooked with other fruits as Banana
and Peach, and dairy products, they, too, are excellent
material for jam, jelly and conserve. Yes, Blackberries
are alkaline in reaction.

Blackberry Jam

1. Gather the fruits in dry weather, allow half a
pound of good brown sugar to every pound of fruit, boil
the whole together gently for an hour, or till the Blackberries are soft, stirring and mashing them well. Preserve
it like any other jam.

2. Collect the fruits when fully ripe, wash and cook
them for one half hour. Add half their weight of moistened
sugar and cook the mixture 10 minutes. (Mrs. V. L.)

BLADDER CAMPION—*Silene Vulgaris*

Synonym: Cowbell.
Habitat: Meadows, waste places.
Part Used: Leaves.
Collection: When 3-4 inches high.

They may be cooked with other greens or included
in soups.

One variety called Wild Pink, *S. Virginica* (L.),

whose flowers are scarlet to deep crimson (those of the Bladder Campion are white), was considered by the Indians somewhat poisonous and by one medical authority as an anthelmintic (worm-expeller).

BLUEBERRIES—*Vaccinium Myrtillus* (L.)

Synonym: Bilberry, Whortleberry.
Habitat: Dry slopes of hill tops.
Part Used: Leaves and fruits.
Collection: Midsummer, when fruit is in full bloom.

"It seems a pity we take Blueberries so much for granted," said newspaper columnist Hazel Andrews, some years ago. How true! The humble Blueberry may well boast of its many virtues. To be sure it offers a most satisfying Summer dessert and represents a free-for-the-asking product of Nature's own vast garden. The leaves and twigs possess medicinal properties. An abnormally functioning kidney tract is soon remedied by prepared infusions. Moreover, it is little realized that the leaves yield Myrtillin, a substance of unknown composition which is now known to reduce blood sugar as does insulin. The fruits tend to act as a new fashioned "blood purifier," such action depending upon the blood-fortifying minerals as calcium, phosphorus and iron, and one other, equally as important as these three, namely, manganese. The latter acts as a catalyzing agent in behalf of the blood stream; that is, it helps to conduct into the blood stream the Blueberry's mineral content, and thus enhances the assimilation of these minerals.

Preparation: The fresh fruits are well reputed for their food values, best eaten uncooked and without sugar. They are also preserved and included in pies and pastries.

Each ounce of fresh Blueberries contains: Calcium, 7.5mgs., Phosphorus, 610 mgs., Iron, 0.0123mgs. The fruits also contain appreciable amounts of Vitamins B₁ and C.

Jellies are best made when prepared with sour Apple.

Any excess of the berries should be sun-dried (or attic-dried) and later in the Fall may be included in puddings and cakes. Allow 10-12 days for complete drying and the berries will resist decay or mold. And for the immediate future one may freeze the fruits, storing them in plastic bags.

Spiced Blueberry Jam

2 pounds Blueberries, 6 cups sugar, 2 teaspoons cinnamon, 1 teaspoon cloves, 1 teaspoon allspice, 1 cup bottled pectin.

Wash and crush Blueberries; add sugar, cinnamon, cloves and allspice. Bring to a full rolling boil. Add pectin; boil hard 2 minutes. Remove from heat. Skim. Pour quickly into hot sterilized jelly glasses. Cover with melted paraffin. When cool, put metal covers on glasses.

Spiced Blueberry jams are sometimes made in combination with fresh Peaches and provide an interesting addition to the jam cupboard.

The Indians harvested large quantities of Blueberries both for themselves and to sell. They dried them on raised scaffolds of rush mats, like Currants or Raisins, which they somewhat resemble. In the winter they liked to cook them with dried sweet Corn, sweetened with a little Maple syrup. They also cooked them with wild Rice and venison, and also incorporated them in a "sweet bread" as is done today with muffins.

BRAKE FERN—*Pteris Aquilana* (L.)

Synonym: Bracken, Wa-ra-be (Japanese).
Part Used: Young coiled sprouts, or tops.
Habitat: Wet woods.
Collection: Spring. The tops or sprouts are gathered up

to one foot of the stem growth and while they are still tightly drawn together into a chicken "fist," as it were. At this stage they are quite tender and rather brittle so that they can be snapped off about 3 inches below the curled top.

Preparation: It has been suggested that the vegetable be soaked in water containing wood ashes so that the free tannic acid be removed: "When the cook gets it, he dumps it into a vessel, covers it with water and throws in a quart or so of wood ashes and lets it soak for 24-36 hours. When it has gone through this soaking process the natural tannic acid content has been extracted by the wood-ash solution." Some have found this procedure commendable and have enjoyed it all the more when included in a vegetable salad and seasoned with Olive Oil and herb vinegar. So prepared, Brake sprouts have a flavor closely resembling that of Almond nuts. Another writer believes that the tops should be placed in hot water for a few minutes and then put into a soup. Its flavor, some say, resembles wild Rice. After its 30 minutes stay in hot water, we generally steam this food a few minutes longer before serving.

The coiled sprouts may also be put into a soup stock. The Indian women thickened their Brake fern soups with freshly ground flour and found that the resultant flavor resembled wild Rice.

"Hunters are very careful," said Huron H. Smith, "to live wholly upon this when stalking does in the spring. The doe feeds upon the fronds and the hunter does also, so that his breath does not betray his presence. He claims to be able to approach within 20 feet without disturbing the deer, from which distance he can easily make a fatal shot with his bow and arrow."

It remains for the Japanese to beat this plant at its own game and make it pay back a little for the many evil things it does; he evens the score by eating it! Ask any intelligent Japanese if he

knows what "Wa-ra-be" is, and he will immediately close his eyes
in a satisfied Oriental grin and tell you all about it and how they
make use of it in Japan. You find that the Japanese vegetable man
goes to the woods and pastures, or to the waste ground along the
highway, or even into the vacant lot next door, when the bracken
stems are shooting up out of the ground in the spring.

While it is in the tender stage with the top not more than a
foot above the ground is the growth stage when the vegetable man
snaps its head off, dropping the curled, tender stalk-end into his
basket.

Soon he has a basketful of tightly curled, woolly, brown stem-
tops and these he carries off to the market where his countrymen
soon find it displayed for sale under the Nipponese name of "Wa-
ra-be," a spring plant to be used in salads and in other ways.

The cook now chops it up fine and puts it into vegetable
salad, with salad dressing and all the rest, and it becomes "Wa-ra-be
salad." He may take part of it and put it in with a mess of spinach
to which it imparts an almond-like flavor.—*El Comancho*, in *Nature
Magazine*

"The presence of nectar-producing organs of Brack-
en is scarcely known," said the *American Botanist*. "They
occur on the fronds on the lower side of the leaf. The
secretion is very abundant during the unfolding of the
young frond. So abundant is it, in fact, that large beads of
the limpid fluid may be seen from a distance, resting
on the nectaries or running down the petiole. . . . Handling and tasting the secretion shows it to be syrupy and
very sweet. The sugars saccharose and glucose are present. Here as in analogous organs and other plants, the
exudation is quite independent of bleeding pressure.
Leaves which have been broken off continue to produce
nectar for several days, provided, of course, that they
are kept in fair condition."

Dr. John Lindley tells us (in *Flora Medica of* 1838)
that in the Canary Islands a "miserable" sort of bread
is made by mixing the flour obtained by grinding the
long, creeping roots with Barley meal.

The early herbage may be substituted for Hops
when making an herb beer.

BROOKLIME—*Veronica Americana*

Synonym: Water Speedwell.
Habitat: Clear ponds, brooks and springs.
Part Used: Upper half of plant.
Collection: Late Spring to mid-Summer.

Wash the herb quickly in cold water before serving.

Brooklime has long been considered a salad plant, is definitely a valuable antiscorbutic, and is used as a flavorful substitute for Watercress. The Spring leaves of this hardy, fleshy perennial are mild and succulent, have a slight pungent taste, and for best results should be eaten with a fresh vegetable salad.

"The herb," suggests Fearing Burr in his book of 1865, "may be propagated by dividing the roots and setting the plants in wet places, according to the natural habitat. It will thrive well when grown with Watercress."

BUCKBEAN— *Menyanthes Trifoliata* (L.)

Synonym: Marsh or Water Trefoil, Bogbean.
Habitat: Marshes and bogs.
Part Used: Roots, herb.
Collection: Spring.

The Scandinavians cook the creeping, jointed roots, which they gather in early Spring, and eat them together with root vegetables. The powdered roots are sometimes used in Lapland to make a bread.

In a scarcity of Hops, this herb has been used in the north of Europe to give a bitter taste to beer. Two ounces will supply the place of a pound of Hops.

BUGLEWEED—*Lycopus Uniflorus* (L.)— *Lycopus Sessilifolius*

Habitat: Wet meadows and moist sandy and peat areas.
Part Used: Tubers (roots).

Collection: Spring.

The tubers may be steamed alone or cooked with other root vegetables. Cut in half-inch lengths, they may be added to soups and stews during the last few minutes of cooking.

GREAT BULRUSH—*Scirpus Validus*

Habitat: Ponds and marshes.
Part Used: Roots and pollen.
Collection: The roots in Fall and early Spring. The pollen from June to September.

The thoroughly dried roots, ground to a fine powder, have been incorporated into a mixture of bread flours. And, it is claimed, "the tender part or the base of the stem, is eaten fresh by the Indians of the Northwest."

Allied Plant: Salt-Marsh Bulrush—*Scirpus Maritimus*
Dr. William Withering, of Digitalis fame, related in the 18th century that the English poor used much of it in times of scarcity, for their bread and broths.

BUNCHBERRY—*Cornus Canadensis* (L.)

Synonym: Dwarf Cornel.
Habitat: Deep, rich woods.
Part Used: Ripe berries.
Collection: August.

This perennial is only 5-6 inches high and often may go unobserved, although it is generally found growing in profusion. Being somewhat insipid and not at all juicy like other fruits, the bright red berries should be incorporated with other berries or fruits when preparing a jelly or conserve. Be sure to strain the finished product to remove the large fruit stones.

In Scotland it is called the "plant of gluttony" because of its supposed power of increasing the appetite. It is said to form part of the winter food of the Eskimos.

BURDOCK—*Articum Lappa* (L.)

Synonym: Burrs, Beggar's Buttons.

Part Used: Early leaves and roots, and stems of the first year's growth.

Collection: The leaves and roots in Spring and early Summer, washed carefully. Since they abound throughout the Summer, they should be washed and dried and saved for Fall and Winter. The stems of the first year's growth, with the "elephant-ear" leaves, are collected in mid-Summer.

Do you know that ubiquitous, unkempt fellow, a certain Mr. Burdock who is to be found in every waste field? The first year of his life produces a rosette of ground-hugging, large, dull green leaves about 1-1½ feet long; the second year, Mr. Biennial Burdock is still, alas, the same ugly duckling grown to the exuberant height of 4-5 feet bearing purple-topped fruits or burrs, which years ago bad little boys would throw at good little girls. And just as you cannot judge people by outward appearances or a book by its cover, so it is not fair to cast reproach on friend Burdock or accuse him of being a "noxious pesky weed." On the other hand, when he does appear in your garden as an unwelcome guest, do remember that the roots of the first year's growth collected in the Spring are a good source of food, and collected in the Fall, an important ingredient in blood purifying remedies, where boils and skin and kidney diseases are indicated.

Prepare the stems by steaming like Asparagus, in as little water as possible, and season with a little herb vinegar or Lemon juice. Save all remaining liquid, which, plain or sweetened, must be considered as food, as valuable as the prepared stems.

Says one nutrition authority, "Of the most important composite drugs, Burdock (*Articum*) and Jerusalem

Artichoke (*Helianthus tuberosus*) have the highest inulin content (not insulin), so that in view of the low cost
of the raw material the Burdock root is used also as a
source of inulin, which some time ago gained some importance in industrial chemistry for the production of fruc-
tose and which for a time was used in medicine in the diet
of diabetics."

An inexpensive way of preparing a much-needed
organic fertilizer is thus given by Thomas Green: "The
herb being burnt green between the time of flowering and
seeding, in a hole made in the ground, without suffering
the flame to escape, 3 pounds of ashes produced 15 ounces
of very white alkaline salt, as good as the best potash."

Gerard says, in his *Herball* of 1597, "The stalks of
the clot-burre before the burres come forth, the rindle
peeled off, being eaten with salt and pepper, or boiled
in the broth of fat meat, is pleasant to be eaten."

Peter Kalm in his *Travels of North America*
(1772) says, "The Governor (in Ticonderoga, N.Y.)
told me that its tender shoots are eaten in spring as
radishes, after the exterior part is taken off."

Burdock Beer—("Bitters")

Take a quartful each of the fresh roots of Burdock,
Wild Sarsaparilla and Spikenard, *Aralia racemosa*, scrub
them clean, slice lengthwise and cut them in half. Boil
them in 6 quarts of water, down to 2 quarts, strain and
when a little cool, add a pint of molasses, or a ½ pound of
sugar, with yeast sufficient to make it work. As soon as
the fermentation commences, it may be drunk. Allow
fermentation to go on for 3 or 4 days. Continue as a
drink until health is restored. It is a good article for
cleansing and purifying the blood.

CALCULATION ON CHEMICAL COMPOSITION

	Water	Nitrogen	Ash	Potassium	Calcium	Sodium	Magnesium	Sulphur	Phosphorus	Silicon	Chlorine
Potatoes	750	3.4	9.5	5.8	0.3	0.3	0.5	0.6	1.6	0.2	0.3
Sugar Beets	815	1.6	7.1	3.8	0.4	0.6	0.6	0.3	0.9	0.2	0.3
Turnips	720	1.8	6.4	2.9	0.7	0.6	0.2	0.7	0.8	0.1	0.3
Carrots	850	2.2	8.2	3.0	0.9	1.7	0.4	0.5	1.1	0.2	0.4
Burdock	738	5.6	10.5	4.3	1.1	0.2	0.9	0.7	0.9	0.1	—

(After Nitobe, Ma. J. Ph. V. 69, p. 416.)

WILD CALLA—*Calla Palustris*

Synonym: Water Arum.
Habitat: Bogs and swamps.
Part Used: The roots. Ripe seeds.
Collection: Fall. Both the roots and seeds must be dried
  for several months before using.

Lindley tells us that, according to Linnaeus, the rhizomes (roots) are made into a kind of bread called Missebroed in Lapland, where it is held in high esteem. This is performed by drying and grinding the roots, afterwards boiling and macerating them till they are deprived of their acridity, and then they are baked like other dough mixes.

The powdered roots may be used in making bread and "herb cookies," being generally prepared like Jack-in-the-Pulpit.

(WILD) CARAWAY—*Carum Carvi* (L.)

Synonym: Kummel.
Part Used: Early leaves. Roots.
Habitat: Waste ground, clayey soil.

In Portland, Oregon, there stands a statue dedicated to the worthy Sacagawea, guide and interpreter for Lewis and Clark, famed explorers of the Northwest. It is recorded that it was she who first introduced the tasty edible Carums (Caraway roots) to these white men, and "carrying her tiny infant on her back, she travelled afoot for hundreds of miles of the roughest mountains, plains and deserts, and by her knowledge of wild foods, contributed greatly to the success of this daring expedition."

Caraway roots are still valued as food substance by the Snake, Shasta and Ute tribes, though under different names—Kash, Yampa, and, more popularly, Ipo, being a corruption of Apio (Celery) and somewhat resembling it, too. Today, it still holds true, I point out to my usually skeptical herb class, that these young, tender Parsnip-like roots are truly delectable as a pot herb or stew constituent (the coarse outer skin being first slightly removed).

Again we turn to the writings of John Parkinson, 17th century English botanist: "The roots of Caraway being boiled may be eaten as Carrots and by reason of the spicie taste doth warme and comfort a cold weak stomache helping to dissolve wind, and to provoke urine, and is a very welcome and delightful dish to great many." You, too, will discover why Caraway roots "while young and tender are by many esteemed a delicacy" when prepared and eaten like Parsnips or Turnips. The late Spring leaves, either fresh or dried, may be incorporated in most vegetable salads as an eatable garnish. Include the tender leaves in your stews and soups.

As a culinary ounce of prevention, Caraway serves much in the same way as most members of the *Umbelliferae* (umbel bearing) family, Anise, Celery, Dill and Fennel. These cousins not only aid the proper digesting of such starchy though nourishing foods as Cabbage, Turnip and Potatoes, but what is more important they are a decided factor in preventing the possible formation of catarrh along the alimentary canal. Bakers of rye, pumpernickel or Swedish bread will invariably add a sprinkle of Caraway to the dough.

CARPET-WEED—*Mollugo Verticillata*

Habitat: Vegetable and flower gardens.
Part Used: Overground portion.

This slender, diminutive herb may be steamed or cooked as a pot herb.

WILD CARROT—*Daucus Carota* (L.)

Synonym: Queen Anne's Lace, Bird's Nest.
Part Used: The roots, seeds.

This herb is the wild prototype of our table Carrot. If it is found in rich soil, the root is sweet and most palatable; located in sandy, hard soil, it is small and hard.

It is best served steamed or cooked in a little water and, cut into inch lengths, added to a soup or a stew.

The seeds serve as seasoners for soups, stews and baked fish; and fresh or dried make a fair substitute for Anise or Caraway seeds.

CATTAIL—*Typha Latifolia* (L.)

Synonym: Cossack Asparagus, Swamp Bulrush.
Habitat: Swamps, marshland.
Part Used: Root stalk. Lower leaf stem. Young shoots and fruiting flowerheads (spikes). The down.
Collection: Collect the root stalks in the Fall, lower leaf stems during August; the spikes while still green. The young shoots are collected in Spring while still green, and the down when the flowers are fully matured.
Preparation: The central portion of the root stalk is mainly starch and after it is collected and completely dried, it is easily ground into fine meal and used like friend Arrowleaf. The early settlers of Virginia ate the cooked roots and were fond of them. One writer claims that competent chemists find the Cattail's food value nearly equal to that of Corn or Rice.

The inner portions of the root and stem are cut into 1 or 2 inch segments and cooked in soups or stews. However, we have found that the young stems, i.e. those collected in Spring, when cut 10-12 inches from the root and the outer rind peeled off, may be added to a vegetable salad.

When the first young shoots appear in Spring, they are rather whitish and crisp, and therefore may be used as an Asparagus substitute. They are usually served as a cooked vegetable. The mildly marshy odor is quickly dispelled by warm water .

A treat is in store for the enterprising kitcheneer who would like to make a bread or cakes from the pollen heads or down of this swamp-dweller. It will take about 20 to 25 good-sized pollen heads to yield a small-sized bread. However it is advisable to mix an equal portion of pure whole-wheat flour, so that uniformity and adhesiveness are more easily obtained.

Cattail flour, especially of the pollen, it is reported, contains protein, sulphur, phosphorus, carbohydrates, sugar and oil.

The heavy, matted roots attain considerable size and they are fairly rich in starch and sugar. The Iroquois Indians formerly dried and pulverized the starchy roots, which yielded a sweet-tasting flour from which excellent bread and pudding were made. Hard-pressed for food during War I, the German people followed the example of the Iroquois Indians and the lowly cattail was a boon to many a hungry Teuton family. Cattail flour is similar in composition to rice and corn flour and it is highly nutritious. The Indians discovered still another use for the fleshy roots. When macerated and boiled, a syrup of an excellent flavor was produced which was commonly used by the Iroquois Indians on corn meal pudding and as a sweetening for other favorite Indian dishes. Cattail roots are said to contain as high as thirty per cent of sugar and starch. With its great variety of uses, it seems strange that the cattail has not been utilized commercially in America where large, heavily-infested areas occur in many sections. Little investigational work has been done on the subject but the necessities of war gave considerable impetus to investigation along this line, although little is known concerning methods of handling a crop of cattails. When harvesting facilities are afforded and milling methods developed, we may witness the utilization of large areas of swampy lands for the production of cattails. Who knows but that bread, biscuits and other products of cattail flour may some day form a regular part of our diet?—Albert A. Hansen, *Nature Magazine*

Members of our Herb Club have also prepared "quite palatable and amazingly delicious" pollen pancakes.

Big Food Yield Seen From Cattails

Had any cattail cookies today? Bought any cattail window drapes or stuffed a pillow with soft cattail fibres?

There is interesting farm news from the Cattail Research

Center of Syracuse University's department of plant sciences. Dr. Ernest Reed, chairman of the department, established the Center this year after six years of preliminary research demonstrated the surprising number of uses of this common plant that grows throughout most of both the warm and temperate regions of our planet.

Leland Marsh, chief investigator of the project, has discovered so many uses of the cattail that it is within the realm of possibility that within a decade there will be commercial cattail farms. Marsh's research shows that one can get a larger crop by cultivating the cattail than by depending on the wild growth. It can be grown on regular farm land provided the land is irrigated.

Yields are fantastic. Marsh discovered he could harvest 140 tons of rhizomes per acre near Wolcott, N.Y. That represents something more than 10 times the average yield per acre of potatoes. In terms of dry weight of cattail flour, the 140 tons of roots would yield approximately 32 tons!

Long before the Spaniards began civilizing the Indians with gun powder, the red men had been using cattail in various ways. Especially in the spring, the Indians dug the starch-filled, bulbous roots and used them in making soups.

They dried the rhizomes, ground them and used the product as flour. Records tell of hungry Virginian settlers boiling the young blossoms for soup. Indian squaws lined papoose baskets with the soft down from the blossoms. Pioneers put a wick through the strong stems and used them as candle molds.

Half a century ago when the fever of political campaigns ran high and torchlight parades were a regular part of campaign strategy, country lads dipped the cattail's sausage-shaped heads in coal oil and used them for torches.

For perhaps 15 or 20 million years, cattails have been growing on our planet. In the prehistoric days when man first began to feel the urge to express himself creatively, he used the tall, lance-like leaves and arresting flower spikes as artistic motifs. The old Italian masters often painted a cattail in the hand of Christ with thorns.

Cattail farming will be important when industry begins to use the products that come from the rhizomes, leaves and fluff. Dr. Reed believes that the world's food problems can be partly solved by growing cattails when one considers that a yield of 140 tons of roots per acre means approximately 32 tons of flour, far ahead of the yield now considered possible from wheat, rye, oats, millet or maize.

The starch content of the roots is sufficient so that cattail flour can be used as a substitute for cornstarch. Furthermore, the Research Center has proved that the flour can be fermented and produce ethyl alcohol. Each year there is increased demand for this alcohol in anti-freeze and as an inexpensive industrial solvent.

Soft fibers from both blossoms, stems and leaves are produced by treating them with chemicals. The fibers can be used in many of the ways in which jute is used; stuffing furniture and making burlap and webbing. Marsh has also discovered a way to make an adhesive from the stems.

He has demonstrated that the fluffy flowers can be pressed and made into efficient sound and heat insulating material. The small seeds produce oil and after the oil is extracted, the meal is nutritious cattle and chicken feed.

The project at Syracuse began in 1947 when Leland Marsh, as an undergraduate from Wolcott, N.Y., began his studies in the university's department of plant sciences. Marsh had more than an academic interest in cattails because he is a partner in a company which furnishes cattails for caulking barrels and for the manufacture of rush furniture.—*News Report*

CHOKECHERRY—*Prunus Virginiana* (L.)

Synonym: Wild Cherry.
Habitat: Banks of brooks.
Part Used: The fruits.
Collection: Late Summer.

Chokecherry fruits are generally made into a jelly, and flavored with citrus fruits and Peppermint, yield a more distinctive flavor. Such doing will often inspire the homemaker toward more creative experiments, as it were, with our native fruits. Prepare your jelly with Apple.

The dark red fruits are somewhat astringent, enough to pucker the mouth; however, this slight astringency disappears when the fruit is cooked.

Our New England Indians employed this method of preserving this food: The fresh fruits were pounded, stones and all, between two flat stones and dried on flat layers of Birch bark. They were stored for the winter months, then to be used as were their dried Blueberries.

BIRD CHERRY—*Prunus Pennsylvanica*

Synonym: Pin Cherry.
Habitat: Border of woods.
Collection: Early Summer.

The bright red fruits are slightly sour and may be eaten uncooked, preferably, or cooked. The small trees bear plenty of cherries with which to prepare a sauce, preserve, or jelly.

RUM CHERRY—*Prunus Serotina*

Synonym: Black Cherry.
Habitat: Banks of brooks and rich woods.
Part Used: The ripe fruits.
Collection: August-September.

The fruits are dark purple to shiny black and possess a juice that is pleasant though slightly bitter and of a vinous flavor.

Do eat them uncooked, or prepared as a sauce or jelly.

CHESTNUT—*Castanea Dentata* (L.)

During the past thirty years the American Chestnut has almost completely disappeared from the New England scene. Its fate is well known, the result of its almost complete destruction by an incurable ravaging bark disease (or blight). However, both the Chinese and Japanese varieties have been introduced in recent years and are reported to be doing very well in their new environment. Orchards of the trees have been planted not only in the warmer climes of the country, but also here in New England and other northern States and in Ontario, Canada.

The Chestnuts that are consumed today in the United States are imported from Italy and Spain (*Castanea sativa*).

George M. V. Wantz of Westminster, Md., reported to the Editor of *Horticulture* that "Japanese chestnuts are worth while and produce a good crop of nuts. They make good eating and they make a very good show with their burrs especially when they turn brown, many remaining on the branches the great part of the winter."

Contents: Calcium, Phosphorus, Potassium, Sulphur, Magnesium. Fat—7%, Protein—11%. Best eaten with uncooked or non-starchy vegetables.

1. *Dessert Chestnuts*: Roast them well, take off the husks, dissolve 4 oz. of sugar in a wine glass of water and add the juice of a lemon. Put the Chestnuts into this liquor and stew them over a slow fire for 10 minutes, add sufficient orange-flavor water (or orange juice) to flavor the syrup; grate lump sugar over them and serve quite hot.

2. *Water Chestnut*: "If the nut, when fresh, is grated and used like fresh corn, with milk, eggs, salt and pepper to make a baked pudding, it is excellent and nutritious. It tastes so like corn pudding that American visitors at my house were always deceived by it."—B.S. Allen, in *Horticulture*.

HORSE CHESTNUT—*Aesculus Hippocastanum*

Unless the poisonous principle is completely removed from these nuts, they are a forbidden, dangerous item of food. (The toxic principle, aesculin, is of service as a sunburn preventive.)

S. A. Barrett, in his *Material Aspects of Pomo Culture*, describes for us the Pomo Indians' method of removing the toxic aesculin:

The large nuts of the Buckeyes are first hulled by removing the thick, fleshy, outer coating. Then the brownish skin is peeled off. These nuts are then boiled in a basket by means of hot rocks. This cooking makes them very mealy. They are next ground or stirred up into a sort of flour. This flour is then sifted and the finer portion is leached in a sand-lined basin. The coarser parts of this Buckeye flour are molded with the hands into balls or lumps; these are placed in a coarsely woven Tule basket which is lowered into the running water of a stream where it remains for a considerable time in order to leach out the "bitter taste" which, of course, means the poisonous element of the fruit (i.e. the aesculin). In either case the resultant product is ready to eat without further cooking. [It is interesting to note that the Pomos' method of leaching the nuts is quite similar, almost step by step, to the specifications of Lord William Murray's patent (early 1700's) for extracting starch from the Horse Chestnuts.]

The *American Botanist*, in 1902, gave another method of removing the poisonous principle from the nuts: "According to a recent report, a way has at last been found to utilize the Horse Chestnut as food. The nut is rich in starch and albumen and contains some sugar, but a certain resin has made it inedible, if indeed not poisonous as is currently believed. By the new process the nut is powdered and the resin removed by alcohol. The resultant meal is said to be rich in food value, and to have an agreeable taste."

From Hooker's *Botany*, 1873, we learn that the seeds, properly prepared, "are given to broken-winded horses. Roasted they are used as coffee and fermented, they yield a spirituous liquor, which yields alcohol by distillation. The young aromatic buds have been employed in place of the Hop in the manufacture of beer."

CHICKWEED—*Stellaria Media*

Habitat: It is quite common in gardens.

Part Used: Upper leaf portion.

Collection: From early Summer to late Fall, May to September. Mulched with a thin cover of leaves, Chickweed will live through the Winter and still be eatable.

Preparation: Herb or leaves are eaten uncooked as salad greens.

In England it is a common practice among pig raisers to give to the very young animals suffering with the disease known as white scour, a large amount of a Chickweed and other herbs rich in iron.

CHICORY—*Chichorium Intybus* (L.)

Synonym: Wild Endive, Blue Sailors.
Habitat: Waste places. Sandy soil. Roadsides.
Part Used: Early Leaves. Roots.
Collection: The leaves in early Spring, the roots in Summer. Dehydrate any excess and save for the future. The roots should be cut immediately into thin strips, dried and properly protected against mold.
Preparation: The leaves should be eaten uncooked in a salad to which is added vegetable oil and herb vinegar; they may also be steamed or incorporated into a soup. The early Spring roots may be cooked and eaten as a warm vegetable, or cut, cooked in a soup or stew.

Since they contain no constipating tannic acid and no heart-affecting caffeine, the Summer-collected roots have for centuries, especially in Europe, been roasted and brewed as a substitute for coffee. If they are gathered before the stems shoot up, they are also edible, for, when thoroughly dried, they may be finely ground into meal with which to prepare bread or cookies.

Intybus refers to the common synonym, Wild Endive, and more especially to the country of Hendibah, Asia, where the vegetable is native. It is sold today in French markets as Barbe de Capucin, in allusion to the toughness of a Friar's Beard (or beard of a Capuchin monk).

The early Romans, thousands of years ago, so wrote the scribes Virgil, Ovid, and Pliny, ate the young Chicory leaves as a vegetable and in salads. True, the Romans then knew nothing of the chemical analysis or food value of Chicory leaves, but if they were suffering with a kidney or liver ailment, these leaves constituted a greater portion of their vegetable greens diet. Moreover, the root is steeped as a worthwhile medicine for stomach and kidney disorders. So great was the demand for Chicory in the late 1800's that notwithstanding its cheapness, it was often in its turn adulterated with roasted Wheat, Rye, Acorns, and Carrots.

The beginner, wrote Fearing Burr in 1865, will enjoy the eating of Chicory if its leaves are first blanched. He offers the following method: "Before using as a salad, the plants are blanched, either by covering with boxes a foot in height, or by strips of boards 12-14 inches wide, nailed together at right angles and placed lengthwise over the rows. They are sometimes blanched by covering with earth; the leaves being first gathered together, and tied loosely at the top, which should be left exposed to light."

When the leaves are properly blanched, they will be of a delicate, creamy white. When they are a foot high, they will be ready for use; and as soon as they are cut, the roots should be removed, and others brought forward to succeed them. In cutting, take off the leaves with a thin slice of the crown to keep them together. When washed and tied up in small bundles of a handful each, they are fit for dressing. But it is better for your health to eat the leaves in their original green state, and if possible, unblanched.

CHUFA—*Cyperus Esculentus*

Synonym: Nut Grass, Ground Almond.
Habitat: Rich soils. Muddy brooksides.
Collection: Fall or early Spring.
Part Used: The nut-like tubers ("chufas") clustered about the base of the plant. Strung and dried, they will keep for a long period of time.

One must be very careful when gathering small, bulb-like Chufas, for they are rather fragilely attached to the roots. It is recommended that one dig well around and beneath the roots of the plant, at least 10-12 inches deep, the better to locate the radical tubers. Furthermore, they may not be located at first by the collector, and "if the plant is not lifted carefully, they break off, remaining underground to start just that many new plants."

Chufa tubers are tender and sweet and have a nutty, Almond-to-Filbert flavor. They may be eaten untreated or roasted like Chestnuts. Not only were they highly prized by our Indian friends, as a food source, but the plant was cultivated in our South and in Europe for these tubers; and today they are sold in the markets of Spain, Italy, and the Mediterranean countries. (One informant relates that Chufas were also advertised in seed catalogues.) According to John Milton Fogg, Chufa tubers are used in Cuba, Spain and other hot countries to make an orgeat. An orgeat is a syrupy drink made from Almonds (originally from Barley) and a water prepared from orange flowers.

Allied Plant: Coco Grass, *Cyperus rotundus.* This is our Southern variety whose nutlike tubers are used like the New England species.

CLOVER (RED)—*Trifolium Pratense* (L.)

Habitat: Native to the temperate zones.
Part Used: Early leaves. Dried blossoms.
Collection: The leaves are collected in Spring, the blossoms when in full bloom, but before they turn brown.
Preparation: We have found the leaves to be a most suitable vegetable insert and Lettuce substitute for cheese sandwiches. At home, they are included in a cole slaw of the native produce—Amaranth, Trefoil and Lambsquarters, et al.

A health tea (tisane) may be prepared by steeping Clover blossoms with Mint and Dandelion leaves or with culinary herbs. Sweeten with honey. This is not only recommended for those abstaining from tea and coffee which contain the harmful caffeine; many who are on a "reducing diet" will find this tea just enough to fill in that empty gap between meals.

A short while ago Mr. James Lee, a student of Worcester Academy, told me that the Chinese people both in their native country and here in Worcester find excellent food value in the leaves of our common Red Clover (*Trifolium pratense*).

In his commentary on Pomo culture and available foods, Barrett relates that in aboriginal times, "Clover was extensively used as a food, and the appearance of the succulent young leaves in the Spring was the signal for special Clover feasts. The people moved out into the fields and reveled in the abundance of these greens, eating great quantities as they gathered them, and bringing them back to the village by the basketful. So quickly did the people devour these greens that it was not unusual for them to be afflicted with bloating similar to that sometimes found among horses and cattle in the Spring."

CLOVER (SWEET)—*Melilotus Officinalis* (L.)
CLOVER (WHITE)—*Melilotus Alba* (L.)

Synonym: Melilot, Sweet Lucerne.
Habitat: Roadsides. Poor, sandy soil.
Part Used: Leaves. Fruits.
Collection: The leaves are gathered before the flowers appear; the fruits, just before maturity.
Preparation: The leaves may be substituted for Red Clover, and also used in soups and stews. However, to use this herb for a bean soup, we have preferred to utilize our excess of dried leaves and fruits which we had previously dehydrated and stored in the attic.

The Yellow or Sweet Clover is closely related to the Red Clover. On a warm day as you pass by this plant, you cannot help but note the sweet vanilla-like odor that fills the air. I well remember my grandfather gathering the young shoots which were later to be boiled like Asparagus. Then later in the Summer we would collect the small pea-like fruits which were used in stews and soups together with garden Peas and Beans and with other wildings. Of course, you will want to make a sachet of the flower heads. Just be sure that you do collect them just before they are fully opened, and when they've been carefully dried, then they are ready for milady.

Mrs. Dana tells us in her 1898 book, *How to Know the Wild Flowers*, that the the flowers of White, Sweet Clover served as "flavoring in Gruyere cheese, snuff and smoking tobacco, and to act as camphor when packed with furs to preserve them from moths, besides imparting a pleasant fragrance."

It was announced that a new chemical has been discovered in Sweet Clover. Said the news report: "Announcement of the proceedings of the Mayo Clinic, Rochester, Minnesota, mentions the discovery of a new chemical in Sweet Clover, *Melilotus alba*, which was traced to the eating of spoiled Sweet Clover. The Wisconsin Agricultural Experiment Station has completed a seven-year study of clots lodging in the heart or lungs and in thrombosis. The only practical remedy up to now has been heparin, a liver extract, whose drawback is that it often makes patients ill. Sweet Clover seems to have no such ill effects and the Mayo report states that it may replace heparin in general use. The advantages of this drug are its effectiveness, its prolonged action, and its cheapness."

CORN SILK—*Zea Mays*

The Chippewa Indians made use of the silk of Corn as a further food source. Called "corn hair," it was dried before the fire and put in broth to season it. The Corn Silk was said to thicken the broth slightly as well as to impart a pleasing flavor.

A brief quote from my *Kitchen Medicines*: "Salvage the yellow silk of Sweet Corn, dry it well and store in a tin can. It is used by the laity and pharmacists as a diuretic in cystitis and in all disorders of the kidneys and bladder . . . . For home use, a teaspoonful of the finely cut silk is steeped in a cup of hot water for 15 minutes. One such cupful carefully strained is drunk four times a day."

CRAB APPLE—*Malus* Varieties

Synonym: Sweet-scented-, American Crab Apple.
Habitat: New England, westward and southward.
Part Used: The near-ripe fruits.
Collection: Late Summer.
Preparation: The Indians, who made use of these tart Apples, collected them in early Fall and stored them for the Winter period. By Spring, the fruits had lost much of their acidity and were either syruped, jellied or made into cider.

Although these acid fruits cannot be eaten raw, they should be of excellent service to the enterprising homemaker, who will find it an easy chore to transform these fruits, plus Blackberries or Raspberries, into a most delicious jam, jelly or pickle.

Mother baked three or four dozen of the "crabs" on a Friday during the picking season. To sweeten she used honey instead of white sugar, and Wild Caraway seeds and powdered Sassafras bark as seasoning.

Friend Chef Pierre tells me that he seasons Crab Apple jelly with a judicious pinch of powdered Cloves, Ginger or Peppermint.

1. *Crab Apple or Apple Jelly*: Wash 2 pounds of sound crab apples or tart apples. Cut out blossom end. Slice crosswise of fruit in ¼-inch slices. Put fruit in pan with 1 quart water. Cook, covered, about 5 minutes and then drain in cheesecloth bag, taking free run juice. Return pulp to kettle and add 1 quart water, bring to boil and cook gently, covered, for about 10 minutes. Drain in jelly bag or cheesecloth square. Mix juices: there should be 2 quarts juice. Strain through 4 layers of

cheesecloth. Put juice on to boil and reduce to half its volume or 1 quart. Add 3 cups sugar to reduced juice (1 quart) and stir to dissolve. Boil rapidly to jelly test (220°). This point should be arrived at not less than 3 or more than 5 minutes after sugar is added. Remove from heat, skim well and pour at once into clean dry glasses, to within ¼-inch of top of jar. Seal with small amount of paraffin. Makes about 4 or 5 6-ounce glasses.

2. *Spiced Crab Apples*: Select sound crab apples uniform in size. Do not pare them. Make a spiced syrup by heating together 1 quart of vinegar, 6 cups sugar, 1 tablespoon each of cinnamon and cloves and 1 teaspoon each of mace and allspice. When cool, add crab apples, and heat slowly, being careful not to burst fruit. Let stand in syrup overnight, pack cold into clean jars, and fill to within ½-inch of the top with syrup. Process in hot water bath for 20 minutes. (Note: If a deeper color is desired add a few drops of red coloring to syrup.)

CRANBERRY—*Vaccinium Macrocarpon*

Synonym: Large-, American-, Bog Cranberry.
Habitat: Bogs.
Part Used: Ripe fruits.
Collection: September-October.
Preparation: According to Oliver P. Medsger, in his *Edible Wild Plants*, the "Pilgrims learned from Indians how to prepare the fruits for the table. The berries kept so long without decay and were prized so highly by the colonists that, according to the early settlers of Massachusetts, 10 barrels of them were shipped across the ocean as a gift to King Charles II . . . .The colonists called the vine 'craneberry' because the blossoms are shaped like the head and neck of a crane. Col. James Smith, who was captured by the French and Indians at Fort Duquesne in 1775, wrote later that he had seen Cranberries which grew in swamps and were gath-

ered by the Indians when the swamps were swollen. These berries were about as large as rifle bullets, of a bright red color, and of agreeable flavor, though rather too sour of themselves, but when mixed with sugar had a very agreeable taste."

The fruits generally are not used fresh, but are stewed to prepare a sauce and jelly, and are also frozen, being stored for future occasions. Invariably the formula for preparing sauerkraut includes the Cranberries. They are also added to pies, puddings, and to sherbet.

Cranberries freeze successfully, either dry-packed or syrup-packed. Dry packing is easy. Just pick over the Cranberries, discarding any that are soft or imperfect. Then wash, drain and place them in moisture-resistant containers. Seal and freeze. Likewise, the firm berries, when growing in their natural habitat and protected by snow, often remain on the vines all winter.

Cranberry Sauce

Those who like homemade cranberry sauce may want to can their own product. Just pour the hot sauce into glass canning jars (pint or quart), adjust lids, and process in a boiling water bath for 15 minutes.

Cranberry Conserve

Still another product you can put up at home is a jellied conserve of cranberries, raisins and oranges. A jar of this, incidentally, makes a nice Christmas gift. The ingredients for conserve are: 2 pounds of cranberries; 1 cup of seedless raisins; 2 oranges; 3 cups of sugar; 1 pint of water. Wash the fruits, peel oranges and discard any seeds. Combine fruits and orange peel and chop together. Add sugar and water. Boil, stirring constantly, for half an hour, or until the jelly stage (220°) is reached. Pour at once into hot clean jelly glasses and seal with paraffin, or put into glass jars and seal.

Cranberry Relish

4 cups raw cranberries; 1 orange, quartered and seeded; 1 lemon, quartered and seeded; 2½ cups sugar, or honey.

Put cranberries, orange, lemon through food chopper. Add sugar and mix well. Chill in refrigerator until ready to serve. Will keep indefinitely.

Cranberry Sherbet

4 cups cranberries; 2½ cups of water; 1 tablespoon gelatin; 2 cups sugar, or honey; ½ cup cold water; ⅓ cup lemon juice.

Cook cranberries and water until skins pop open. Strain, add gelatin, softened in cold water, and sugar. Heat until sugar is dissolved. Cool and add lemon juice. Freeze until firm in refrigerator.

HIGH-BUSH CRANBERRY—*Viburnum Opulus* (L.) Var. *Americanum*

Synonym: Cramp Bark.
Habitat: In thickets, along streams.
Part Used: The ripe fruits.
Collection: September to November.

The Viburnum is often cultivated in gardens as a mere ornamental and while the shrub may be good for lawn or park its fruits have needlessly been overlooked as a source of fresh fruit.

This species is called High-Bush Cranberry since its sharply acid and succulent fruits taste very much like the Bog Cranberry, to which it is not at all related. The bright red fruits are treated like real Cranberries and served as a delicious sauce or piquant jelly, care being taken to strain, to remove the large stones.

By all means, do prepare with Orange and Lemon peels and note the difference.

Wild Cranberry Jelly

This jelly is made with wild High-Bush Cranberries. Use one-fourth as much water as cranberries. Boil 20 minutes. Put through a sieve. Bring juice to boiling point and add one-half as much sugar as there is juice. Boil 5 minutes. Pour into sterilized jars. Cover with one-quarter inch of paraffin.

ROCK CRANBERRY—*Vaccinium Vitis-Idaea*

Synonym: Cowberry, Mountain Cranberry, Red Bilberry.
Habitat: Dry, barren or rocky soil of high hills and mountains.
Part Used: The ripe fruits.
Collection: Fall to early Winter.

The red Blueberry-like fruits are too acid to be eaten as is. They are generally prepared in Cranberry fashion as a sauce or jelly for meats and poultry.

CUCUMBER ROOT—*Medeola Virginiana*

Habitat: Moist, rich woods.
Part Used: The root system.
Collection: Early Summer to Autumn.

The tuberous roots were eaten by the Indians as a cooked food, although they should be steamed to a suitable softness, sliced and included in soups, stews or warm vegetable plates just before serving.

The cuke roots may also be preserved by pickling in an herb vinegar.

BLACK CURRANT—*Ribes Americanum*
RED CURRANT—*Ribes Rubrum*

Habitat: Wooded areas.
Part Used: Fruits.
Collection: When ripe.
Preparation: When Dr. Dorothy Taylor, the British

food expert, visited Worcester during October, 1943, she stated in an interview that one way which contributed to beating the food shortage due to the war was her woman's ingenuity for finding makeshifts—namely, using a native fruit to supplant the Oranges which had been imported from the United States. "We looked around," said Dr. Taylor, "and found that black currants were the highest source of vitamin C grown in England. So we made a syrup from them for babies under 5 months and a puree for children under 2, and fed them that."

Currants furnish excellent acid fruits for preserves, jellies, sauces and pies.

Dry any excess by placing the fruits on trays and heating them in the sun or an oven. Turn them over occasionally, to expose the other side to the heat, until thoroughly dried. When using them, add enough hot water to render them to any consistency suitable for jelly or sauce.

Cool Currant

Another tangy, fruity flavor for summer drinks made its bid in an English import: Ribena Black-Currant Syrup, rich in Vitamin C.

Currant-Mustard Sauce

Currant jelly with its rich, clear color and special flavor has many uses in meals the year round. For instance, it's an excellent complement to meats and makes a tasty sauce for ham.

Here's how to make the sauce—Place equal parts of currant jelly and prepared mustard in the top of a double boiler. Heat the jelly and mustard over hot water until the jelly has melted down. Serve hot. This currant jelly sauce brings a delightful tang to a routine dish.

Black Currant Jam

Take 2 pounds of fruits that are thoroughly ripe, and clean from stalks. Bruise them well in a bowl and stir in 1½ pounds of sugar. Place this in a pot and boil for ½ hour. Skim the top if necessary and stir the mixture often.

Black Currant Wine

Pick and squeeze currants when fully ripe. To one gallon of juice add six quarts of water, and to each gallon of this mixture add three and a half pounds of brown sugar. Mix well together and strain. Put into a cask, and let it be ventilated till it shall have passed the active or vinous fermentation, when it may be well corked. As it will improve by age, it may be well to let it stand undisturbed for years unless wanted for medical purposes.—*An old recipe*

DANDELION—*Taraxacum Officinale*

Part Used: Leaves, flowers, and roots.

Habitat: Grassy places, fields, meadows.

Collection: Leaves in Spring, flowers in Summer, roots in Fall.

Preparation: The leaves, when young and undried, are best eaten as a salad green and any excess may be dried and stored for future use. When fully grown, they are too bitter for table use but these may be dried and a warm infusion of them will serve admirably as a stomachic or bitter tonic in dyspepsia or indigestion. For which purpose, Dandelion's generic name *Taraxacum* attests: *taraxos*-internal disorder; *akos*-remedy.

If they are to be cooked as a Spinach substitute, it is better to steam rather than cook them. To flavor, add grated Garlic, Onion, Lemon peel or Basil.

The North American Indians called Dandelion

"strong root." They used the leaves for greens only in the Springtime in the same manner in which the colonists did. They cooked the cut leaves with a little vinegar made from Maple sap.

The older leaves and the accompanying flowers and stems may be utilized by preparing a wine or health beer, plus Nettle and Yellow Dock leaves, Orange and Lemon peels.

The dried root, roasted and grated, makes a suitable substitute for coffee, than which it is far more healthful, not containing the harmful, heart-stimulating caffeine of coffee.

One vegetable farmer in New Jersey, it is reported, has cultivated several acres of Dandelion, as well as the usual Beets, Potatoes, etc.

Compare the food values of a pound of Dandelion and Lettuce, fresh and uncooked:

	Dandelion		Lettuce
Protein	12.3	Grams	3.8
Fat	3.2	Grams	0.6
Carbohydrates	40.0	Grams	9.1
Calcium	849.	Mgs.	194.
Phosphorus	318.	Mgs.	63.
Vitamin A	61,970.	I.U.	5,060.
Iron	14.	Mgs.	3.4
Thiamin (Vit. B_1)	0.85	Mgs.	.14
Riboflavin	0.65	Mgs.	.26
Niacin	3.8	Mgs.	.6
Vitamin C	163.0	Mgs.	57.0

Here is a European report on the uses of the Dandelion. It is from Thomas Green's *Universal Herbal*, 1823.

"Early in the Spring, while the leaves are hardly unfolded, they are not an unpleasant ingredient in salads, and are said to be a powerful antiscorbutic. The French eat the (early) roots and the leaves blanched, with bread and butter. At Gottingen, the roots are roasted and substituted for coffee by the poor, who find that an infusion prepared in this way can hardly be distinguished from that of the coffee-berry. . . . When a swarm of locusts had destroyed the harvest in the island of Minorca, many of the inhabitants subsisted upon this plant."

YELLOW DOCK—*Rumex Crispus* (L.)

Synonym: Curled Dock.
Habitat: Waste places and roadsides.
Part Used: Tender leaves.
Collection: Spring.

The early Spring greens are a bit too coarse for the ordinary palate and are generally served steamed. When young and tender, they should be steamed for 3-4 minutes in the water which adheres to the leaves. Season with herb vinegar or Lemon juice. As usual the greens may be either cooked or included in a pot herb or in a soup.

Food values per 100 Grams (3 ounces): Vitamin A about 20,000; Protein 2.1%; Mineral Content 0.95%.

ELDER— *Sambucus Canadensis*

Habitat: Wet places, sides of brooks.
Part Used: Blossoms, fruits.
Collection: Blossoms when not fully expanded. Fruits when ripe.
Preparation: Although the dark purple berries are the more popular, the creamy, fragrant blossoms that appear in flat-topped clusters may be used also as an ingredient in pancakes and scrambled eggs. (See recipe below). The fully expanded blossoms are generally steeped and drunk for their diaphoretic and stimulant properties in colds and high blood pressure.

Elderberries will be found to be an excellent source of easily obtainable fruit material, readily processed without difficulty into jelly, preserve, and wine. As a jelly, they may be used alone or with Apples, Grapes or Raspberries. However, when preparing a jam or sauce of the Elderberries, stew the fruits a longer period of time than when using fresh fruits. Our fruits are generally canned with Lemon and Orange peels, wild Grapes and honey, and stewed with the ever-present Lemon peels and honey.

The fruits will be found to be plentiful so that a good crop once properly dehydrated in a warm current of air (say, in the attic) will provide a substantial quantity that may be stored for future or winter use as herein described. Be sure, however, to leave the stems on the fruits, which are to be placed on a clean sheet, stems up.

The young shoots of young Elder shrubs have also been used as a substitute for Asparagus. In the Spring when 5-7 inches high they are cut and tied up in small bundles and quickly cooked in hot water.

Elderberry Wine

2 quarts of berries; 3 pounds of sugar; 1 pound of raisins; ¼ ounce of Sweet Flag Root; ¼ ounce cinnamon; ¼ ounce cloves; ¼ ounce ginger.

1. Directions: Boil the ripe fruits, previously crushed, in a gallon of water for ½ hour. Add the sugar and the spices. Boil again for 20 minutes and set aside for 3 days. Add one pound of yellow raisins to each gallon. Let it stand for 100 days. Filter if so desired.

2. Express the juice in some convenient way, wash the pulp and press again. To a gallon of the juice add 3 pounds of sugar and allow to ferment.

Elderberry and Apple Jam

1 quart ripe elderberries; 1 lemon; 3 oranges; 12 large cooking apples; 5 cups of sugar.

Pare and core apples and cook until mushy. Add elderberries, juice of lemon and oranges. Grind the rind of two oranges, and ½ of the lemon rind, then add the sugar, mix all together, and boil for 30 minutes. This is a delicious jam.

The next three recipes are from Alta Garrett Mc-Clanahan and appeared in *Horticulture* magazine:

Fried Elderberry Blossom

"1 cup flour; 1 teaspoon baking powder; ⅛ teaspoon salt; 1 egg; ½ cup milk; 6 clumps blossoms.

"Wash the blossoms, which have been cut with two or three inches of stem. Holding by stem, dip into batter and fry in deep, hot fat."

Elderberry Jelly

"1 cup juice; 1 cup sugar; ½ cup pectin. Proceed as in making other jellies."

Canned Elderberries

"Wash ripe berries and put into preserving kettle. Cover with syrup made of one cup sugar to three cups water. Bring to boil, fill jars and seal. Use for drink with lemon added, or for pies."

Elder Flower Lemonade

Cover the freshly collected flowers with 2 quarts of cold water. Add a lemon cut into quarters, a tablespoonful of malt or cider vinegar, and ⅔ of a pound of sugar. Stir well. Allow to stand 24 hours. Stir occasionally. Strain and simmer the mixture for 15 minutes. Chill one week before using.

The following two recipes are from *The Receipt Book of John Nott, Cook to the Duke of Bolton*, 1723.

Pickled Elder Buds

"Put the buds into vinegar, seasoned with salt, whole pepper, large mace, lemon peel cut small, let them have two or three warms over the fire; then take them out, and let the buds and pickle both cool, then put the buds into your pot, and cover them with the pickle."

Elder Flower Fritters

"Gather your bunches of Elder flowers just as they are beginning to open, for that is the time of their perfection. They have just then a very fine smell and a spirited taste, but afterwards they grow dead and faint; we complain of these flowers having a sickly smell, but that is only when they are decaying; when fresh and just open they have the same flavour, but it is spirited and just the contrary of what it is afterwards. The Elder flowers being thus chosen, break each bunch into four regular parts, lay them carefully in a soup dish; break in a stick of cinnamon; pour to them a wine glass of Brandy (warm wine); and when this has stood a minute or two, add half a pint of Sack, stir the flowers about in the liquor, cover them up, and let them soak about an hour, uncovering them and stirring them about at times to see how they keep moist; put a handful of the finest flour into a stewpan, add the yolks of four eggs beaten, and afterwards their whites beat up to a foam; add some white wine and a little salt, and put in the whites of the eggs last. When the batter is thus made, set a quantity of hog's lard in a stewpan; when it is very hot, fry the fritters.

"The method is this: The Elder flowers are to be taken out of this liquor and put into the Batter, and the quantity for each fritter is one of the bunches of Elder with as much batter as agreeably covers it, and hangs well about it. While they are frying, heat the dish they are to be sent up in, rub a Lemon upon it, now cut, and lay in the fritters as they come out of the pan; strew a little of the finest Orange-flower water over them, and serve them up."

This recipe is from *Godey's Lady's Book*:

Elder Wine Flavored with Hops

"A lady, disliking the taste of spices in home-made wines, was induced to try the effect of flavoring elder wine with hops. The result is one of the most grateful, wholesome and valuable beverages. Its color equals that of the finest claret; and it produces no acidity after drinking, as many home-made wines do. The berries, which must be thoroughly ripe, are to be stripped from the stalk, and squeezed to a pulp. Stir and squeeze this pulp by passing through a sieve or basket; to every gallon of juice, add half gallon of cold water; boil nine gallons with six ounces of hops for half an hour; then strain it, and boil again with three pounds of sugar to the gallon, for about ten minutes, skimming it all the time. Allow to cool, and while lukewarm, put a piece of toasted bread with a little yeast to set it working and put it into a cask as soon as cold. When it has done working, cork it down and leave it 6 months before it is tapped. It is then drinkable but improves with age exceedingly."

ELM— *Ulmus Fulva*

Synonym: Slippery Elm.
Habitat: Native to New England.
Part Used: Dried inner bark.
Collection: Summer.

The Indians used the cut bark as an "extender" and emergency food, and cooked it "with all their animal fats in rendering out the grease. These tribes (Omaha and Canada) have realized that the bark gives a desirable flavor to the fat and a preservative quality, preventing the rendered grease from becoming rancid."

It is reported that the surgeons of the Revolutionary Army of 1776 used the bark as a source of "quick-energy" nutriment and that the soldiers who may have lost their way, supported themselves for 12 days upon a jelly prepared with the bark and that of Sassafras.

George B. Emerson in his *Trees and Shrubs of Massachusetts*, 1875, says that the flour prepared from the bark by drying and grinding is mixed with milk and forms a wholesome and nutritious food for infants and invalids.

When crops failed or long severe winters exhausted food supplies, Indians and pioneers alike were often saved from starvation by the use of Sweet Elm bark. This emergency source of food had the advantage of being available when all other sources of food had failed. The use of Sweet Elm bark as food spread with the early colonies until the day when the vast forests were converted into farm lands.

Slippery Elm bark is recognized in modern times for its soothing properties in cases of irritations of stomach and intestines. The powder mixed with milk is wholesome and nutritious. It is easily digested, and owing to the fact that it absorbs noxious gases, it is useful for inducing restful sleep, when taken at night. It is beneficial for infants and adults who have a tendency to constipation.

Slippery Elm Tea With Egg

1. Beat up an egg with teaspoonful of the powdered bark. Pour boiling milk over mixture and sweeten to taste.

2. Make smooth paste with one teaspoonful of powdered Slippery Elm and small quantity of cold water, then pour on slowly a pint of boiling water, stirring until thoroughly mixed. Flavor with nutmeg or lemon if desired. This tea is excellent in cases of irritation of the mucous membrane of the stomach and intestines.

—The Herbalist Almanac

OSTRICH FERN—*Onoclea Struthiopteris* (L.)
Osmunda Struthiopteris (L.)

Synonym: Fiddleheads.

Habitat: Dense moist thickets, along streams.

Part Used: Young fronds.

Collection: Spring, before the fronds begin to uncurl.

Preparation: Before using, one must first remove the brown scales by wiping them off with a damp cloth, and second, chill them in the refrigerator for a few hours to remove "woodsy" odor. Friend Chef Pierre further suggests that before they are cooked, they should be chilled or steeped in wine plus seasoning herbs, for half an hour.

Naturally, they are to be cooked but do not boil

these delicious fiddleheads; do steam them in as little water as possible. They make a most suitable substitute for Asparagus or cut string Beans.

Ostrich Fern is well known in northern Maine where it is gathered not only for local use but shipped to Boston and to New York markets, However, the fern, being of rather a prolific character, will produce numerous young shoots on the short runners and has so been propagated.

Steamed Fiddleheads may be served cold in a vegetable salad and seasoned with a little Lemon juice. They may also be canned by being simmered for 5 minutes, packed hot into hot tested jars and processed at 10 pounds pressure. Store in a cool, dark place.

SWEET FERN—*Comptonia Asplenifolia*

Habitat: Roadsides, sandy soil.
Part Used: Nutlets. Leaves.
Collection: June-July.

The young nutlets are removed from the burrs either with a knife or thumbnail. As an oft-needed nibble, they are generally available in sterile fields or on roadsides.

The Indians made a practice of lining their Blueberry pails with leaves of Sweet Fern which they claimed kept the fruits from spoiling.

Use the late-Spring collected leaves for your herb tea (tisane). Dry the leaves, and before infusing them, make a test for proper taste. If there is the slightest astringency, use the leaves either for an herb pillow or as a medicinal remedy, and if none, steep a scant teaspoonful of the ground leaves in a cupful of hot water for 3-5 minutes. For extra flavor, add crushed, dried rinds of Lemon or Orange.

SWEET FLAG—*Acorus Calamus* (L.)

Habitat: Swamps, sides of brooks.
Part Used: Upper half of leaves. Roots.

Collection: Leaves in Spring; root in late Summer, or Fall.

Preparation: The young, tender leaves will be found to be a most flavorable asset to a chicken soup or stew. Any abundance should be dried, ground and properly preserved in mason jars—thus providing an excellent source of flavorful greens for winter soups. The roots may be candied by boiling them in thick syrup, à la candied Ginger or Angelica. In Turkey, the roots are made into a confection, which is considered a good stomachic, and is eaten freely during the prevalence of epidemic diseases.

The roots collected in Spring are considered a good substitute for some of the imported spices as Ginger or Cinnamon. They are used fresh or dried as a culinary herb, to flavor meats and fish, stews and soups. The leaves alone, wrote Nicholas Culpepper, in the 17th century, "having a very grateful flavour, are by some nice cooks put into sauce for fish."

The spicy roots supply extra zest to an herb or spice vinegar but should not be considered the sole ingredient. Do include at least 2 or 3 other "naturals" as Wild Garlic, Mints, Sassafras, Barberry, Lemon rinds, and other garden-grown culinary herbs.

It is important to note that in addition to the strong, aromatic, volatile oil there is another active constituent called Choline. It is this substance that is most actively engaged in helping the body to counteract the excess of, and the possible ill effects of, the artery-hardening cholesterol.

Here is a recipe from Mrs. Frank Taylor which appeared in *The Herbarist*, publication of the Herb Society of America.

Candied Flag Root

"The root should be dug in the fall; washed and scraped and peeled, then cut as thinly as possible with a sharp knife, and simmered for several hours—probably 6 or 7—changing the water whenever one thinks of it. I usually let it stand in cold water overnight, then drain it and cook it in syrup made of 2 cups of sugar to ½ cup of water, until it crystallizes, stirring often.

"Turn it out on waxed paper and separate the pieces as soon as it is cool enough to handle. It really has to be pried apart with a knife. I wish I could tell you the exact amount of root I use in this quantity of syrup, but have never measured it. I use a 2-quart saucepan.

"As this is a nibbling candy, it can be put up in small quantities, in cellophane bags or small boxes, or small glass jars. It is much liked by the old folks who remember it."

GALINSOGA— *Galinsoga Parviflora*

Habitat: Gardens.
Part Used: Upper half of the plant.
Collection: Whenever possible.

Use as a pot herb in stews and soups.

WILD GARLIC—*Allium Canadense* (L.)

Synonym: Outlaw of the Lily family.
Habitat: Moist pastures.
Part Used: Top bulbs and stems.
Collection: Mid-Summer.
Preparation: The stems and whole bulbs are generally
    accepted as a suitable substitute for the store
    bought variety. They are eaten cooked or uncooked,
    and pickled "secundum artem."

As to the food and culinary aspects of Mr. Garlic, it is a must ingredient of pastrami, chicken cacciatore, and many European dishes. Defenders of Garlic's culinary potency have long maintained that besides adding zest to their meals the pungent vegetable has brought to them added health and happiness. "While the flavor of this plant is very strong," Huron Smith tells us, "the Indians use it in soup and have always accounted it a valuable wild food. . . . In 1674 when Marquette and his party journeyed from Green Bay to the present site of Chicago, these onions (cloves) formed almost the entire source of food."

Garlic, like the other members of his family, Onion, Leek, and Chives, offers to you an excellent source of Vitamin C, and a fair amount of Vitamins A, B and G. It abounds in the minerals of sulphur, iron and calcium.

Garlic should always be considered a most valuable medicinal—both as a preventive against possible disease and then as a curative when needed. Daily doses taken in any way possible will help to fight diseases of the nose and respiratory tract, and have been recommended for persons with high blood pressure. It has been much used as an asthma remedy, and as a worm syrup. Moreover it is an excellent intestinal antiseptic and an especially good stimulant to the digestive system.

Want to partake of our bonodorous friend? I suggest your trying out this gradual-dose experiment with which I've found much success for my family and my friends. Our practice has been to make further use of the recently collected bulbs so that we may produce a continual supply of greens which keep tempting us with their tangy, chlorophyllated elements and vitamins. Do this also with store-bought Garlic.

Procedure: Separate a whole Garlic into the respective cloves (some 6 to 8) and plant in rich, well-drained soil, or in such soil that is adapted for the growing of Onions. Soon enough, scallion-like tops will have grown 6 to 8 inches high, high enough to be cut and ready to be collected. Cut close to the original clove, about one inch above the soil, and then you may use the green tops either as is, mixed with other greens as Celery, Lettuce or crisp uncooked Spinach, or else you may incorporate them in cole slaw, although I prefer the open caesar-type salad. Include them whole in your vegetable salads; cut, in cole slaw or Potato salad; diced, in cream or cottage cheese. In either case, be sure to include Cress (either Water or Garden Cress), and friend Parsley. In cold salads, these two, Parsley and Cress, will do the honor in disguising quite effectively the possible odors of the Garlic oil.

It is recommended that ⅔ of the flower pot or container be filled with such soil in which the Garlic grew. Water well and allow to drain. To fill the other ⅓ of the pot, mix well equal parts of garden soil with composted material, either with or without egg shells and a sprinkle of finely ground Dandelion and Burdock leaves.

Garlic has had a long and interesting history from time immemorial. According to the Talmud, in Baba Kama, the eating of Garlic served many purposes. It satiated hunger, it kept the body warm, it brightened up the face, it killed parasites in the body, it fostered love and removed jealousy. The Egyptians, however, worshipped it, and Romans gave it to their laborers to impart strength, and to their soldiers to excite courage. Their game cocks were also fed with Garlic previous to fighting.

The Hindus have used Garlic for the past 3,000 years. The early Egyptians and Hebrews considered Garlic a food endowed with divine properties—and so it is really. The Irish have used it for centuries for curing coughs, and Pliny, the Roman naturalist, attributed curative powers to Garlic in respiratory and tubercular ailments. The Latin and French peoples, and the Romans and Greeks, have realized its subtle flavor for centuries. Aristophanes, the ancient playwright, mentions it many times in his comedies.

It is a fact that Bulgaria, up until that madman Hitler took over that nation, led in proportion all other European nations in centenarians, who lived in small villages or mountainous districts and led regular but rather primitive lives. Indeed, they attributed their longevity to the diet of fresh vegetables and fruits and daily doses of sour milk and Garlic, cultivated and wild.

Charles F. Saunders reminded us in his *Useful Wild Plants of the United States and Canada* that although it may be true than no plant has a worse reputation with the dairy farmers, Mr. Garlic must be credited with a most worthwhile economic use. "Why not use this bit of adversity," says Saunders, "as adversity should be used: to further one's purposes? Garlic can become a valuable spring pasture for cattle and sheep. Why not pasture such meat-producing animals on it until they are fat and then put them up in a feed lot for from 2 to 3 weeks before selling them? It is said that it requires a little more than 2 weeks completely to remove the odor from the meat. Perhaps Garlic pastures may become valuable to the fat-stock grower if managed properly.

"Garlic and sin will likely be with us until this old world goes up in smoke or becomes a frozen ball."

WILD GINGER—*Asarum Canadense*

Synonym: Canada Snakeroot.
Habitat: Rich, shady woods.
Part Used: The roots.
Collection: Spring.

The Chippewa Indian regarded the root as an appetizer and put it in any food as it was being cooked. Today we consider the therapeutics of the roots of Wild Ginger as being carminative, diaphoretic and stomach bitter.

It is primarily employed as an ingredient of a native spice vinegar and of mixed pickling spices. It should be substituted for and candied like Ginger.

GOLDEN CLUB—*Orontium Aquaticum*

Synonym: Tuckahoe.

Habitat: Swamps, bogs and ponds.
Part Used: The roots and seeds.
Collection: The roots in Spring and Fall; the seeds in
     mid-Summer. Dry both for at least a month before
     using.

The bulbous roots are edible only when cooked and
then are served like other starchy vegetables; while the
seeds, resembling beans when dried, must be briskly
boiled twice in hot water, then are eaten as Peas or Beans.

The Swedish botanist, Peter Kalm, noted in his
journal of 1749 the Indians' preparation and use of this
foodstuff: "The Indians pluck the seeds, and keep them
for eating. They cannot be eaten fresh or raw, but must
be dried; the Indians were forced to boil them repeatedly
in water, before they were fit for use; and then they ate
them like peas. . . . Sometimes they employ these
seeds instead of bread. The cattle, hogs and stags are
very fond of the leaves in Spring."

SWEET GOLDENROD—*Solidago Odora* (L.)

Synonym: Anise-scented Goldenrod.
Part Used: Leaves and flowers, collected in mid-
     Summer.

Another "beverage" plant that makes a suitable tea
substitute is none other than our dear friend, Sweet Goldenrod, but don't let the mention of Goldenrod bring un-
comfortable visions of being afflicted with hay fever.
When you have identified this proper Goldenrod, collect
the leaves when the plant is in bloom and use them fresh
or dried, with Peppermint leaves, as an after-dinner summer tea. One writer has said, "What has been said about
the Dandelion is equally true of the Goldenrod and As-
ters. They would be considered highly ornamental in a
garden if they were not so common in the fields." And I
might add, highly medicinal, too, for not only did the
American Indian employ this common herb as a "cure"

for sore throat and for pain in general, but today it is equally recommended by herbalists as a diaphoretic in colds, coughs, and as an aid in rheumatism. For, does not the generic name, *Solidago*, mean "I make Whole," i.e., heal?

Said Dr. Johann D. Schoepf (1788): "Here we were introduced to still another domestic tea-plant, a variety of *Solidago*. The leaves were gathered and dried over a slow fire. It was said that around Fort Littleton, Penna., many one-hundred pounds of this Bohea-tea, as they call it, had been made as long as the Chinese was scarce. Our hostess praised its good taste, but this was not conspicuous in what she brewed."

Statement by Frederick Pursh, globe-trotting botanist, in 1816:

"The flowers, gathered when fully expanded, and carefully dried, give a most agreeable substitute for tea which for some time has been an article of exportation to China, where it fetches a high price."

I find recorded in my notes that the Western Indians who planted corn and often made long journeys far away from their villages, knew that it was time to return and gather their crops when the Goldenrod came into bloom."

Herb Tea: Teaspoonful to a cup of hot water. Do use the leaves and flowering tops of all the native Goldenrods.

GOOSEBERRY—*Ribes Oxyacanthoides*

Synonym: Groser, Feverberry.
Habitat: Thick, wet woods.
Part Used: The fruits, leaves.
Collection: The fruits when fully ripe, reddish purple, in mid-Summer, July-August. The leaves, in Spring, when tender.
Preparation: The young and tender leaves may be in-

corporated in a fresh salad or cole slaw. The fruits, however, are of greater economic importance, being used in sauces, pies, jams, chutney, etc. They offer a constant supply of palatable wild-growing fruits which are far superior to the cultivated species. They are prepared like Currants, being members of the same family.

Of the many varieties of Gooseberries, the above is the most satisfactory for all purposes and may be even transplanted in the Fall into one's garden, where, if properly mulched with vegetable compost or grass cuttings or both, it will be found to be resistant to Gooseberry mildew.

Herbalist Gerard (1597) says, "The fruit is much used in divers sawces for meats and used in brothe instead of Verjuyce, which maketh the brothe not only pleasant to taste, but is greatly profitable to such as are troubled with hot, burning ague." Thus is applied the synonym, Feverberry, for which reason the fruits are also prepared as a warm tea for a feverish cold, a teaspoonful to a cup of hot water, etc. The French make a wine of them, too, which is taken cold as an appetizing tonic and warm as a fever-breaking remedy for colds and winter fevers.

The other synonym, Groser, refers to the family name *Grossularia*.

The following recipe is from Henry Hartshorne's *Household Cyclopedia*, 1871.

Green Gooseberry Cheese

"Take six lbs. of unripe rough Gooseberries, cut off the blossoms and stems, and put them in cold water for an hour or two; then take them out, bruise them in a marble mortar, and put them into a kettle and heat, stirring them till tender; then add 4½ lbs. of lump sugar pounded, and boil till very thick and of a green color, stirring all the time."

GOOSEGRASS—*Eleusine Indica*

Habitat: Sandy, poor soil.
Part Used: Seeds.
Collection: Mid-Summer.

The seed or grain of the Goosegrass is so large that it was at one time used to make a poor grade of flour. In some of the poorer sections of Europe and Asia, it is said that Goosegrass flour was made (and perhaps still is made) from a selected variety of the weed.

The seeds, dried and cleaned, may be added to soups and stews.

WILD GRAPE—*Vitis* Species

Synonym: Grapevine.
Habitat: Gravelly roadsides.
Part Used: Leaves. Tendrils. Fruit.
Collection: Leaves in Spring, the tendrils in early Summer, and the fruits when ripe.

Being slightly laxative and diuretic, Grapes of all kinds have long been recommended for their cleansing properties. This therapeutic action is desirable when it is necessary to increase kidney function by decreasing the acidity of the urine and eliminating uric acid from the body.

The Grapevine has been known to man from time immemorial and was much used by the ancient Egyptians and Hebrews more than 6000 years ago. Grapes were not brought from Europe to America. Leif Ericson found them here and called the land "Vineland." Edward Winslow wrote of New England in 1621 that "there are grapes, white and red, and very sweet and strong also."

The corkscrew tendrils make a tasty nibble, and also, a large quantity may be pickled in an herb vinegar later to be included in a cole slaw. The early leaves should be gathered in the early morning, washed in cold water

and used either as cooked(i.e. steamed) Cabbage or as
the jacket for meatball fritters. Cut into inch squares,
and seasoned, they may also be included in soups and
stews. The square may be seasoned with grated Lemon
peel.

Eaten fresh, the fruits contain dextrose sugar,
malic and tartaric acids.

With store-bought Concord Grapes and the wild
growing species, we have prepared sauces, jellies and
marmalades combined with Lemon and Orange peels,
and these home-made delicacies are now standard with
scores of herb-minded friends.

If a wine is in order, it should be drunk only in
moderation and then only as a tonic appetizer to increase and to effect better digestion. Grape wine is an
excellent base with which to prepare an herb wine when
it is to be used to flavor cooked meats or as a wine sauce.

Spiced Wild Grape Jelly

1 peck wild Grapes, not quite ripe; 1 quart vinegar,
not too strong; ½ cup whole pickling spices (Cinnamon,
Cloves, etc.); 12 cups sugar.

The Grapes may or may not be taken from the
stems. Add the spices (tied in a bag) and the vinegar,
and cook until soft. Strain through a jelly bag. Boil the
juice 20 minutes, add the sugar, which has been heated
in the oven, and boil until the jelly stage (220°) is
reached. Pour into sterilized glasses and cover with paraffin.

Herb Jelly

To make Thyme-flavored Grape jelly, tie 2 teaspoons of dried Thyme or a small bunch of fresh Thyme
in a cheesecloth bag, and add it to the Grape juice before
boiling. Remove it before adding the sugar. Very good
with pork and game.

The Jelly Pulp

The pulp in the jelly bag of previous recipes may be used to make very appetizing jams and butters, good for spreading on the children's bread, for filling tarts, for making steamed and baked puddings, and for many other purposes.

Grape Wine

Express enough of the fruits to yield ⅔ of a gallon. Wash the pulp again and then express enough juice to make ⅓ more. Add 3 lbs. sugar, allow to ferment several days.

GROUNDNUT—*Apios Tuberosa*

Synonym: Hopniss, Wild Potato.
Habitat: Sandy roadsides.
Part Used: The tubers. Fruits. Seed pods.
Collection: The tubers after September. The fruits when mature.

The ever-travelling Groundnut is a poor and honest relation of the popular Soya Bean. The early Pilgrims were taught by the American Indians to respect the wilding as a source of nutriment. (Perhaps these early settlers caller this food "Happiness" rather than Hopniss.) In the sandy soil attached to the root system are found the edible tubers, or small potatoes, growing in a rather long chain, somewhat like a string of enlarged beads. For this reason, they were called "rosary roots" by the French Jesuit Missionaries in Canada, who observed how the small tubers grew as the Indians gathered them. These are the "potatoes" that Sir Walter Raleigh's expeditions took back to England.

The tubers contain protein, natural sugar and starch, and minerals, thus being a rather valuable food article. Washed clean they may be steamed or baked when first harvested, cooked with other vegetables and in soups, or dried and preserved for future use. To dry them for use during winter, one author (name unknown) stated: "They are first boiled and peeled, then they are threaded like beads on a string and hung up to dry. When dried they are very hard, and when required for use, they are pulverized in a mortar before cooking."

We have eaten much of these wild Potatoes and found them as edible and satisfying as the cultivated variety.

The seedpods are also to be used and are prepared by cooking them with the seeds (fruits) in them.

Henry David Thoreau has written in *Walden*: "Digging one day for fish worms, I discovered the groundnut (A. T.) on its string, the potato of the aborigines, a sort of fabulous fruit, which I had begun to doubt if I had ever dug and eaten in childhood. I had often seen its crimpled red velvety blossom supported by the stems of other plants, without knowing it to be the same. It has a sweetish taste, much like that of a frost-bitten potato, and I found it better boiled than roasted. This tuber seemed like a faint promise of Nature to rear her own children and feed them simply here at some future period."

Nicholas Perrot (circa 1660) is said to have been the first Frenchman to record the native foods (weedy edibles) of the Indian tribes of the Potawatomi, especially the Muskodaisug, on the east shore of Lake Michigan. While travelling through the Potawatomi Indian country, according to Huron H. Smith, Nicholas Perrot presented the following description of the potatoes: "Some are as large as an egg, others are the size of one's fist, or a little more. They boil these in water by a slow fire, during 24 hours; when they are thoroughly cooked, you will find them an excellent flavor, much resembling that of prunes."

Botanist Peter Kalm (1772) claimed that the roots of the Groundnut were comparable to the tubers of the

Irish Potato. He noted that not only did the Delaware Indians eat heartily of Hopniss; the "Swedes ate them for want of bread and in 1740 some of the English ate them instead of potatoes." They also prepared a wholesome bread from the tubers.

One writer in the early 1800's offered the suggestion that the Groundnut be propagated by transplanting them to a suitable habitat. Said he, "They will lay up large subterranean stores that the earth will be literally packed with them. Many of the tubers are as large as medium-sized potatoes."

HACKBERRY—*Celtis Occidentalis*

Synonym: Sugarberry.
Habitat: Rich, moist soil.
Part Used: Fruits (berries or drupes).
Collection: Fall.

As the foliage of this small tree begins to turn a soft yellow, the green fruits ripen in Autumn to an orange-brown to purple and remain on the branches all Winter long. The thin pulpy covering is very sweet— and thus its synonym, Sugarberry—and pleasant to the taste.

"It transplants easily from the wild," we read in a newspaper story. "Hackberry does best in rich soil but can be grown on almost any home grounds. It will grow in poor soils, but under such conditions does not attain the height or free-flowing line of a 'contented' tree. Fortunately for the home owner who likes to dig plants from the wild, hackberry is well adapted. The root system is mainly lateral, which means that a good percentage of it can be taken up in a digging operation. Another point in its favor is the fact that it is resistant to drought conditions."

BLACK HAW—*Viburnum Prunifolium* (L.)

Synonym: Stag-bush.

Habitat: Wet hillsides and roadsides.
Part Used: Ripe fruits.
Collection: Fall.

The berry-like fruits of this tall shrub ripen to a dark purple to black, and freshly collected, are incorporated into a jelly, jam or sauce, which are best seasoned with Lemon peel, or with an aromatic herb of your choice.

HAWTHORN—*Crataegus* Species

Synonym: Bread and Cheese.
Part Used: Ripe fruits.
Collection: Early Fall.
Preparation: The bright red fruits are collected when fully mature and even then are still not over-palatable. Of the freshly collected fruits, one should prepare a marmalade or preserve and utilize the still undried peels of Lemon, Orange or Grapefruit. Rosemary and Thyme will add culinary zest and proper seasoning to the finished product.

*   *   *

"The fair maiden who, the first of May,
Goes to the fields at break of day
And washes in dew from the Hawthorn tree
Will ever after handsome be."

—from *Nature's Garden*

*   *   *

New Englanders take full advantage of a heavy crop with which to prepare an herb wine.

HAZEL—*Corylus Americana*

Hazel shrubs average 8-9 feet and have been recommended not only as attractive shrubbery for the home garden but also as a source of nuts, which are called by some "filberts." The nuts are collected in late Summer to early Fall.

Contents: Calcium, Magnesium, Phosphorus, Potassium and Sulphur. Fat—64%, Protein—16.5%.

The nuts are best eaten with acid fruits and green vegetables.

Here is an amusing story from a newspaper report.

"A farmer with a fine stand of hazelnut trees was bedeviled by trespassers during the nutting season. He consulted a scientific friend, and upon his advice placed at conspicuous points the following notice:

" 'Trespassers, take warning! All persons entering the wood do so at their own risk, for, although common snakes are not often found, the *Corylus avellana* abounds everywhere about here, and never gives warning of its presence.'

"He was troubled no more with trespassers.

"(In case you don't know, *Corylus avellana* is the botanical term for Hazelnut.)"

HICKORY—*Hicoria Ovata*

Synonym: Shagbark.
Habitat: Rich, heavy soil. Groves on rocky hillsides.
Part Used: Nuts.
Collection: Fall.

It is best to qualify the Hickory since here in New England, whose rich woods it inhabits, we refer to it as the Shagbark, in the Middle West it is the Shellbark, and in other sections of the country the Pignut and Mockernut.

Hickory nuts are still one of our most abundant native nuts. They ripen and are collected during September to November. The flavor of the nut is very rich and sweet. They should be roasted, cooked in soup or stew, prepared with meats or chicken.

The nuts are high in fat, 60%, fair in protein, 15%.

Donald Culross Peattie, botanist and author, gave a detailed, factual report of the Shagbark Hickory in the *Scientific American*:

"As early as 1640 our Hickory was described by an English botanist. And in William Strachey's *Historie of Travaile in Virginia Britannia* we read of a tree whose nut is 'exceeding hard shelled and hath a passing sweet karnall; this . . . the Indians beat into pieces with stones, and putting them, shells and all, into morters, mingling water with them, with long woodden pestells pound them so long togither untill they make a kind of mylke, or oylie liquor, which they call *pocohicora*.' From this Indian word, evidently, derives the name of Hickory.*

Allied plant: Pignut, *Hicoria Glabra* (which see)

HOLLYHOCK—*Althaea Rosea*

Habitat: Waste compost-rich places, gardens.

Part Used: Early leaves.

Collection: Throughout the growing season.

Preparation: Hollyhock is originally a native of China, where it grows naturally and whence its seeds are imported, but has been thoroughly naturalized in our gardens and environs. Since early days when horticulture was little understood and the choice of esculent vegetables extremely limited, the plants of the Mallow family were chief amongst the more common articles of diet. Even today, the peoples of Asia, especially China, still prepare Hollyhock leaves for their meals—uncooked in salads, cooked in soups.

As permissible substitutes for the more popular Ground and Marsh Mallows, the roots of the Hollyhock are similarly demulcent and emollient, thus being of good service in cough and diuretic remedies.

The generic name, *Althaea*, is derived from the Greek *Althainein*, meaning "to heal."

* From "Shagbark Hickory" by Donald Culross Peattie. Copyright © Sept., 1948 by Scientific American Inc. All rights reserved.

HOPS—*Humulus Lupulus*

Habitat: Moist rich soils. It is also found as a climbing
vine in thickets and along river banks.
Part Used: Young shoots. The fruits (strobiles).
Collection: The shoots in Spring. The fruits (the Hops)
in early September.
Preparation: The young whitish sprouts are gathered
when 4-6 inches high and prepared like Asparagus
or as a pot herb for soup. In the early 1800's
small bunches of the sprouts were sold in markets
under the name of Hop-Tops. At one time, ground
Hops were used as a substitute for baking soda.

The greenish-yellow flowers are the Hops used
commercially in the preparation of beers and ales.

HORSERADISH—*Amoracia Lapathifolia* (L.)

Habitat: Wet places. Clayey soil.
Part Used: Leaves. Roots.
Collection: Only the tender leaves are to be collected in
Spring. The roots are also collected in the Spring
and any excess may be preserved for future use by
covering in sand.
The "5 bitter herbs" said to have been eaten by the
Hebrews during their 8 days of Passover are Horseradish
(or Wild Radish), Coriander, Hoarhound, Lettuce and
Nettle.
The name, Horseradish, refers to the pungency of
the root.
The following is taken from one of the writer's
radio talks:

Horseradish has been employed both as a food and medicine
since the earliest of days. It is considered to be one of the bitter
herbs, (i.e., Chrane and Charosis), eaten by the Hebrews of Ancient Egypt during the Feast of Passover. Throughout the ages it
has been used as a medicine by the herbalist as a cough remedy
and worm expellent.
As a food, Herbalist Gerard some 350 years ago recommended

that, "The Horseradish stamped with a little vinegar put thereto, is commonly used for sauce to eate fish with and such like meates as we do mustard." Thus, comparing Mustard with Horseradish, the properties of the latter are found to be the same as Black Mustard, and the active principle is Singarin, producing a volatile oil known as allyl isothiocyanate. Horseradish root produces little odor until one begins to grate it, and that is because this volatile oil does not pre-exist in the fresh state. The bruising of the root causes another ingredient called Myrosin to act on the active principle, Singarin, thus yielding the somewhat acrid volatile oil.

Horseradish root is rich in Vitamin C, yielding 100 units, and proportionally, that's more than Lettuce and Green Peppers can boast of. Furthermore, its medicinal properties must not be overlooked. Even as a seasoning, it performs its duties as a diuretic, stimulant and antiseptic. Taken with oily fish or fatty meat, either by itself or steeped in vinegar, or in plain sauce or seasoning, it acts as an excellent stimulant to the digestive organs and as a spur to complete digestion.

To prepare fresh white Horseradish sauce, wash the root clean and let soak in cold water for 2 hours. Grate the root into enough cider vinegar to make sauce. Want to tone down the biting flavor of a Horseradish sauce? Try mixing in a pinch or two of the ground leaves of either Basil, Dill (and seed) or Oregano.

See also *Horseradish*, Leaflet #129, United States Department of Agriculture, 1965.

For winter use, take up the root systems of this hardy perennial in November, pack them in moist sand or earth, and store in the cellar or in any situation out of reach of frost.

TRUE HUCKLEBERRY—*Gaylussacia Resinosa*

Synonym: Black, High-Bush Huckleberry.

Habitat: Woods, thickets, sandy soil.

Part Used: The fruits.

Collection: Mid-July to September.

Preparation: More attention should be paid by the conservationist and Nature-lover to the Huckleberry in his never-ceasing search for wild growing produce. These fruits are needlessly neglected, despite their abundance in our immediate environs. This neglect may either be due to their improper identification as "poison Dogberries," or even when they are properly identified, their being thought to be "too stony," or too difficult to convert into a food. True, the fruits do contain stony seeds but they are quite delicious, somewhat tangy and sweet. As Maude Gridley Peterson has well put it, "Huckleberries and milk! What recollections of childhood the combination recalls. Bluebirds, robins, crows and bluejays share with mortals a liking for the berries."

The fruits are cooked and are either preserved, jellied or sauced. Strain to remove the seeds.

The genus *Gaylussacia* was so named in honor of the chemist, Gay-Lussac; the specific portion of the Latin name *Resinosa* refers to the fact that the flowers and leaves are densely covered with resinous dots.

ICELAND MOSS—*Cetraria Islandica*

Synonym: Consumption Moss, Iceland Lichen.
Habitat: Bare hills, on the ground amidst rock area.
Collection: Late Summer. When first gathered, it is of a pale or grayish brown color, but after having dried thoroughly, it turns a light gray. Botanically, the plant is a lichen but looks like a moss.
Preparation: It has long been employed in medicine as a demulcent in bronchial affections and catarrh, and as a nutrient tonic for general debility.

It may be consumed either as a mucilage or jelly. To prepare the former, first wash with cold water and stir well a handful in a pint of boiling water, cover and let stand at least 3 hours. Stir, strain and sweeten with honey. To provide extra taste, Lemon or Orange peel may be included. The Moss may also be boiled in milk a few minutes to provide palatable nutriment, this vehicle being a most suitable tonic for children and convalescents.

A jelly may be prepared by first washing a handful of the Moss in cold water and then simmering it in a quart of boiling water until completely dissolved. It has been recommended that for taste there be added the juice of 2 Lemons or a glass of wine and a little Cinnamon. Add also one glass of Honey. Strain and seal.

IRISH MOSS—*Chondrus Crispus* (L.)

Synonym: Salt Rock Moss, Carrageen.
Habitat: On rocks, along the North Atlantic shore.
Part Used: The dried, bleached plant.
Collection: Whenever available.
Preparation: The jelly made from Irish Moss is highly
  nutritious, free from sugar and starch, and thus is
  a most nourishing form of diet especially adapted
  for diabetics and invalids. Being rather insipid the
  Moss should be cooked with milk or seasoned with
  vanilla extract or fruits. Recently, Irish Moss has
  been combined with Sweet Potato to make a gela-
  tine-rich food. The extractive, Carrageen, is used by
  confectionery and bakery firms to prepare low-acid
  content sweets. Manufacturers of chocolate milk
  drink find the extractive valuable as a suspending
  agent.

Irish Moss is also used in "findings" of coffee, to precipitate the excessive, constipating tannic acid, and for this purpose it is far cheaper than using eggs.

Moss Jellied Fruit

Prepare a jelly by boiling for a half hour about a half cup of the Moss in 1½ pints of hot water. Stir occasionally and strain at end of boiling time. About a half pound of mixed fruits will be needed and these include Orange, Banana, Grapefruit, Figs and Prunes. Pour into molds; as the Moss cools and jells, add Raisins and Nuts.

Thin Jells

Irish Moss, generally considered the basic ingredient of many nutritive puddings and jellies, offers the much needed sulphur and iodine food elements to the human body, ill or well.

Irish Moss	½ oz.
Water	3 pints

Boil 15 minutes, stirring occasionally. Express and strain. Flavor to taste. Chill before serving.

Irish Moss	2 teaspoonsful
Milk	1 pint
Honey	1 ounce

Prepare as above.

For further recipes, see under Iceland Moss and Elm.

It should likewise be considered a must kitchen remedy for a variety of ailments. Steeped in a warm Pekoe tea solution and strained when cool, the Moss yields a jelly that quickly soothes and heals a fresh burn or scalding, sunburn, etc.

Mixed with Cucumber juice and/or Quince seed jelly, Irish Moss offers a soothing hand lotion to apply to chafed or winter-chapped skin, although it is much more employed as an excellent demulcent and emollient to allay stubborn coughs due to colds in which case Honey and Lemon juice should be mixed with the Moss jelly.

JACK-IN-THE-PULPIT—*Arum Triphyllum* (L.)

Synonym: Indian Turnip, Wild Turnip, American Wake Robin.

Habitat: Rich, wet and shaded woods.

Part Used: The roots (corms).

Collection: Spring, when the Jacks are in flower.

Preparation: The roots when freshly collected, are intensely acrid. They must be cut transversely and dried for at least 5 months, at which time they are finely powdered, sifted and substituted for wheat flour. "When a small piece of the fresh corm is chewed," states the *American Botanist*, "the mouth feels as if being pinched with countless needles, especially at the base of the tongue. In a very short time this sensation ceases so long as the tongue is held perfectly still, but the least movement renews the prickly sensations that tingle like shocks of electricity. In the course of 20 minutes most of the tingling passes off, but one may feel faint twinges for an hour or more longer."

"We learn," said Huron H. Smith, "that at an early day Nicholas Perrot, who visited the Potawatomi, found them using the 'bear root,' *owassautci'pa*, and told how they could convert this very hot and poisonous root into an edible food. Perrot said, 'An actual poison, if it is eaten raw; but they cut it in very thin slices and cook it in an oven (the pit oven method was found necessary to render acrid and poisonous foods harmless and starchy foods saccharine, and as a preliminary for drying and preserving for winter use) during 3 days and nights; thus by heat they cause the acrid substance which renders it poisonous to evaporate in steam, and it then becomes what is commonly called *cassava root*.'"

Although the English Jacks, in Elizabethan days, yielded a highly valued, nutritious food to those who were well acquainted with the proper procedure of their preparation, it proved to be too blistering to the hands of the poor women who were unfamiliar with the herb's acridity and soon fell into undeserved disuse. However, in Ireland where the plants grow in profusion, the corms, properly treated, have been utilized as a foodstuff to full advantage. The Irish, even today, prepare the Jack powder by grating the corms into water, allowing to soak 1-2 hours, pouring off the liquid and drying the sediment. The resultant powder is stored for at least 4-6 weeks before being used.

JEWEL WEED—*Impatiens Biflora*

Synonym: Touch-me-not.
Habitat: Wet lowlands and swampy areas.
Part Used: Early shoots.
Collection: Spring. Early Summer.

Only the small shoots, less than 4-5 inches high, may be garnered and served at the table. Even at this stage of growth, care must be taken to eat only a handful of this mineral-laden herb at a meal-time. *Always eat Jewel-weed with other vegetables.* If too much of older plants is consumed, the therapeutically-active minerals may cause mild purgation.

JUNIPER—*Juniperus Communis* (L.)

Habitat: Dry hills, limestone areas.
Part Used: Ripe fruits.
Collection: August-September. *Do not collect any of the Juniper in wet areas.* Collected there, the fruits yield a fraction of the desired volatile oil.

Botanist Linnaeus has stated that the Laplanders drank warm teas of the fruits as we do tea and coffee, and that in Sweden, a beer is prepared from the fruits "in great estimation for its diuretic and antiscorbutic qualities."

Some use the fruits to season poultry and meats (as ham); others, to flavor soups (especially pea soup), stews and meat sauce. For each preparation, 5 or 6 berries are sufficient. And be sure to remove the fruits before serving the food.

KNOT GRASS—*Polyganum Aviculare* (L.)

Synonym: True Knotweed, Wild Buckwheat, Nine Joints.
Habitat: Rich waste places, sides of brooks.
Part Used: The closed flower heads containing the seeds.
Collection: Late Summer, when the flower head is com-

pletely pink. The seeds are to be dried and finely ground.

Preparation: The seeds of Knot Grass may be substituted for Buckwheat, thus the common synonym, Wild Buckwheat. Both are members of the same (*Polyganaceae*) family. Powdered into meal they are suitable for cookies, pancakes, and vegetable patties.

The plants may be easily identified by their stems, which are thickened at the nodes, giving them a jointed or "kneed" look. Hence the generic name *Polyganum*, many knees.

Allied Plant: Smartweed, *Polyganum hydropiper* (L.), produces fruits and stems that, if not handled carefully, will produce a mild blistering and smarting and long enough to "cause the careless one to respect this little plant vixen as long as he lives." Aye! *hydropiper* means Water Pepper.

JAPANESE KNOTWEED—*Polyganum Cuspidatum*

Synonym: American Bamboo Shoots.
Habitat: Waste places.
Part Used: The young shoots.
Collection: In the Spring, when 6-8 inches high.
Preparation: The shoots are preferably steamed for 3 or 4 minutes and served as an Asparagus substitute. They may also be cooked with Cranberries to prepare a cold sauce.

LAMBSQUARTERS—*Chenopodium Album* (L.)

Synonym: White Goosefoot, Wild Spinach.
Habitat: Rich soil. Garden "weed."
Part Used: The leaves and fruits.
Collection: The young shoots, Spring-Summer-Fall, when 5-6 inches high and tender. The fruits when mature but still unopened. By all means, do de-

hydrate any excess of the young Lambsquarters, which should be used in future soups, stews, meat-loaf, etc.

Preparation: In the late Spring, the first appearing leaves should be eaten alone *uncooked*, or cooked as an ingredient of hot or cold salad and flavored with a mere sprinkling of Garlic or herb vinegar, or prepared like Spinach. Canned Lambsquarters is a nutritious vegetable substitute, worthy of consideration by both homemaker and conservationist. Several years ago the greens were sold by the bushel at the Reading Terminal Market, in Philadelphia, Pennsylvania.

The ripened fruits, when completely dried, should be ground into flour and used to prepare bread, cookies, etc., as has already been stated under Jack-in-the-Pulpit. The fruits may be used alone or mixed with other grains or cereals.

The dried, unground fruits also provide a plentiful supply of excellent bird seed. Tweety, son Saul's pet canary, seems to thrive on them. In fact, I have known one bird fancier who preferred these soft grey fruits to all others, not only for their nutrient qualities but for their anthelmintic (worm expelling) properties; thus did he save unnecessary expense. Other sources of bird food are the fruits of Ragweed, Plantain and Knotgrass.

Writing in *Organic Gardening*, Dr. G. M. Hawkins states the Lambsquarters "was highly esteemed by the Maori and their kindred as a food, and when made into a drink. That race in the heyday of their vigor, before they were exploited and despoiled by the devastating whites, were the most comely, powerful and happy of native peoples.

"It would be well for the costive, constipated, liver-sick, auto-intoxicated American addicts to catharsis to make Lambsquarters their emblem and pay tribute to it on their luncheon and dinner tables. They might then be freed of their bondage and become candidates for what certain enthusiasts call 'Glorious Health.' "

Note: It is one of the best examples wherein the use of native foods kept the Indians in health. It was supposed by them to be a specific in the treatment of scurvy or in its prevention. Therefore the Potawatomi felt rather duty bound to include it in their diet as fresh salad and Spring greens.

The specific name, *Album*, refers to the singular silver sheen of the leaves, which are whiter than most other common plants.

It is one of the best indicators of good soil, and, if gathered before the fruits appear and cut into smaller segments, may be used as excellent fertilizer.

WILD LETTUCE—*Lactuca Scariola* (L.)

Synonym: Prickly Lettuce.
Habitat: Rich soils of wastelands.
Part Used: The tender shoots.
Collection: Collect in the Spring when 5-6 inches high.
Preparation: Seldom eaten uncooked, the shoots are generally steamed (or pressure cooked) or included in vegetable soups. It is important to note that our cultivated Lettuce, *Lactuca sativa*, is actually derived from this wild species, as is the garden Carrot from the Wild Carrot which is commonly referred to as Queen Anne's Lace.

This plant is greedily eaten by poultry.

Allied Plant: Horseweed, *Lactuca Canadensis*.
Steam the young leaves and tender stems or use them as a pot herb. Horses in particular are fond of the herb, therefore its name.

CORN LILY—*Clintonia Borealis*

Synonym: Cow Tongue.

Habitat: Wet woods.
Part Used: The early leaves, not yet unfurled.
Collection: Spring.

The young leaves, collected in early Spring, lend their Cucumber flavor to a fresh vegetable salad. The later leaves may be included as a pot herb in stews and soups.

POND LILY—*Nymphoea Odorata*

Synonym: Water Lily, Water Nymph.
Habitat: Swamps, still ponds, and marshes.
Part Used: Leaves. Flower buds.
Collection: The tender leaves in Spring; the flower buds while still unopened. The flowers bloom in July and yield a sweet Hawthorn-like scent.
Preparation: After they are washed thoroughly, the leaves may be chopped and cooked in soup and stew or included in meat fritters. The flower buds may be eaten cooked, though they may also be pickled, later to serve as a spiced relish.

Water Lilies are lovely in the garden or in a shallow vase, but how would you like a water lily sandwich? From London comes the story that a certain Reverend W. F. Falloon eats water lilies for strength.

Every morning in the lily season, the 78-year-old Rector, who lives in Kent County, chooses a lily from his goldfish pond and inserts it between slices of bread and butter. He eats this sandwich before breakfast. Sometimes he adds a little jam because, he says, "Water Lilies have no flavor of their own." But the Rector claims the lilies are "very sustaining" and that he can work for 12 to 14 hours on one sandwich. He says: "I've been eating them for 16 years now and I'm not dead yet!"—*News Report*

LINDEN—*Tilia Americana* (L.)

Synonym: Basswood, Lime Tree.
Habitat: Rich woods.
Part Used: Flowers. Sap. Leaves.
Collection: Summer.

Linden flowers and leaves offer a far more healthful substitute for Pekoe tea and after-dinner beverage
for those inclined toward chronic dyspepsia, with the result that the general nervous and digestive systems are
most beneficially affected. To prepare an infusion, steep
a teaspoonful in a cup of hot water and cover 5-6 minutes.
Stir and strain. Sip slowly and drink one such cupful 4
times a day. The tea is helpful also to relieve severe
cramps and nervous or "acid" indigestion. Linden tea is
the nightcap of the French, and such drinking is a practice for all health enthusiasts to adopt.

Tiliae ad mille usus petendae! The Limes demand-
ed for a thousand uses!

LIVE FOREVER—*Sedum Purpureum*

Synonym: Frog Plant.
Habitat: Wet roadsides.
Part Used: Leaves.
Collection: Spring.
Preparation: The leaves are collected when young
     in early Spring, washed in cold water and included
     in a mixed vegetable salad. They may also be
     pickled a day or two in herb vinegar, yielding an
     agreeable relish item, and provide added seasoning
     for cole slaw or cut salad.

BLACK LOCUST—*Robinia Pseudoacacia* (L.)

Synonym: Robinia, False Acacia.
Part Used: Seeds.
Collection: Fall.

The 2-inch-long seed pods contain from 4 to 10
seeds which the Indians cooked with their meats. The
seeds, wrote Oliver P. Medsger, "are slightly acid and
oily and may be used as we use peas and beans. They lose
acidity on boiling and become a pleasant nutritious
food. The pods could be dried and preserved for winter
use when other vegetable food was scarce."

Other portions of the tree contain severely toxic principles. The inner bark of the tree is very poisonous.

YELLOW LOTUS—*Nelumbo Lutea*

Synonym: Water Chinquapin.
Habitat: Ponds
Part Used: Tuberous roots. Seeds. Shoots.
Collection: The roots in Spring and Fall, seeds in Summer, the shoots in late Spring to early Summer.

Long before Columbus arrived, the Indian men of the Tennessee to Mississippi River area had the Lotus under extensive cultivation. The soft tubers, with their characteristic flavor resembling the sweet potato, were cooked for food, while the entire seed pods, still containing the hard round seed balls, were dried to provide rattles or an extra source of nutrient. The ripe seeds were peeled and eaten either uncooked or ground into flour, a practice for the present-day herb-eater to recognize, as well as the eating of the steamed soft roots.

"Most of the Wisconsin Ojibwe," wrote Huron H. Smith, "knew about this favored Wild Potato; and also used the hard Chestnut-like seeds to roast and make into a sweet meal. They cut off the terminal shoots, at either end of the underground creeping root stock, and the remainder is their potato. These roots are similar in shape and size to a banana, and form the starchy storage reservoirs for future growth. They have pores inside, but have more substance to them than the stems. They are cut crosswise and strung upon Basswood strings, to hang from the rafters for winter use. They are soaked when needed and then cooked with venison, corn or beans."

Nicholas Perrot in the 17th century described their preparation: "To eat it, you must cook it over a brazier and you will find that it tastes like chestnuts. The savages are accustomed to make provision of this root; they cut it into pieces and string them on a cord, in order to dry them in the smoke. They put them into bags and keep them as long as they wish. If they boil their meat in a kettle, they also cook this root, which thus becomes soft; and when they wish to eat it, it answers for bread with their meat."

WILD LUPINE—*Lupinus Perennis* (L.)

While it may be true that the ripened seeds of this blue-flowered species are cooked and eaten like domestic peas and that the white Lupine has been extensively cultivated in Europe to give its green herbage as food for the domestic animals, it is too dangerous a plant to be considered as a food source, for there exists a highly poisonous substance in the pods and seeds. However in Italy and France Lupine are cultivated as a meliorating crop in dry barren soil that is so sandy that rarely will Clover or other plants thrive there. It is a legume used as green manure and therefore assimilates the much-needed nitrogen from the air to enrichen the soil.

LOW MALLOW—*Malva Rotundifolia*

Synonym: Cheese Plant, Dwarf Mallow.
Habitat: Rich, garden soil.
Part Used: Leaves.
Collection: Summer.
Preparation: The Cheese Plant is so called because its
    fruit is flat and shaped like a miniature whole
    round cheese. Its common name, Mallow, is de-
    rived from the Greek *Malake*—'to soften,' hence the
    especial qualities of all Mallows of softening and
    healing a diseased area, sore or ulcer. Yes, many
    centuries ago, Pliny broadcast that "whoever shall
    take a spoonful of Mallows shall that day be free
    from all diseases that may come to him." Mallows
    contain three principal constituents, Mucilage, Pec-
    tin and Asparagin, which act as a demulcent and

emollient, in the inflammation and irritation of the alimentary, respiratory and urinary organs. The early leaves are to be included in gumbo soups and stews.

Allied Species: High Mallow: *Malva Sylvestris*
  Marsh Mallow: *Althaea Officinalis* (L.)
  Hollyhock: *Althaea Rosea*
  Okra: *Hibiscus Esculentus* (L.)
The leaves of High Mallow and Marsh Mallow may be substituted for the Low Mallow.

MANDRAKE—*Podophyllum Peltatum* (L.)

Synonym: May Apple, Wild Lemon, Umbrella Plant.
Habitat: Rich, shady woods.
Part Used: Ripe fruit.
Collection: Mid-Summer, July-August, when the plants begin to die and fall to the ground.

The yellow, pear-shaped ripe "apples" possess a somewhat pulpy interior and a taste resembling strawberry. A most desirable marmalade and jelly may be prepared from the fruits, while their juice adds special flavor to a wine and fruit punch. Mrs. C A. Iddings wrote in the *American Botanist* of her jelly-making experiments with large May Apples: "It is fine, a clear and amber color and the flavor delicate and delicious. It has no medicinal qualities and is one more fruit for scarce years."
Cave: Take no chances. Eating too many of the fruits may cause griping and unpleasant after-effects.

The fruit, reported Charles F. Saunders, has "a rank disagreeable odor when green but at the time of maturity is delightfully fragrant, with a perfume hard to define, but combining the characteristic smells of Cantaloupes, summer Apples and Fox grapes . . . As to the edibleness of the fruit, that is a matter of taste; some people loathe it, while others are very fond of it. It ought

not to be condemned, however, on the evidence of unripe specimens, but should be accorded the advantages
based on mature fruit. When ripe the little apples are
yellowish in color and drop into the hand when touched.
The outer rind is rejected by connoisseurs, the portion
eaten being the translucent jelly-like moss that encloses
the seeds. On a hot day this is found to be a refreshing
acidulous morsel by many a thirsty rambler. New England housewives sometimes pickle the green fruit."

In *Nature's Garden* Neltje Blanchan wrote: "Dr.
Asa Gray's statement about the harmless fruit
'eaten by pigs and boys' aroused William Hamilton
Gibson, who had happy memories of his own youthful
gorges on anything edible that grew. 'Think of it, boys!'
he wrote; 'and think of what else he says of it: "Ovary
ovoid, stigma sessile, undulate seeds covering the lateral
placent are each enclosed in an aril." Now it may be safe
for pigs and billy goats to tackle such a compound as
that, but we boys all like to know what we are eating and
I cannot but feel that the public health officials of every
township should require this formula of Dr. Gray's to be
printed on every one of these big loaded pills, if that is
what they are really made of.'"

MAPLE—*Acer Saccharum, Acer Saccharinum* (L.)

The Maple sugar industry here in the North is
the most truly American and the most truly personal of
all industries. It was born as a necessity of food in earlier
times and has remained a great New England tradition.
Wherever the Sugar Maple is found, a bit of New England is found there also, for this tree stands out alone as
one of Nature's rarest gifts. It takes about 12 to 14 quarts
of sap to make a pound of sugar and in many instances
healthy trees produce as high as 15 to 20 pounds per
tree.

Mr. Richard C. Potter, director of the Museum of
Science and Industry of Worcester, Mass., said on a

radio broadcast, "The origin of Maple sugar making takes us into the Indian days of our continent. Long before the white man came to these shores the Indians knew of the secret of the Maple tree. They too, even though their tools were crude, turned the sap of the Maple into sugar and syrup. By skillful use of reed and bark troughs they slashed the bark and collected sap. The squaws brought the sap to a boiling point by heating stones and casting them into the troughs and then straining the resulting syrup through blankets. These Indians mixed sugar with powdered sweet corn when they went on a journey. One of their main uses of this mixture was a sauce for their roasts of venison. Algonquin Indians became quite efficient sugar makers and were then known as 'tree eaters' among their fellows. When the white man came here the fame of the tree that made sweet sugar had already spread to Europe, and one of the first efforts of these settlers was to explore the sugar making secrets of the redskin. He came to settle in one place, and it was important that the tree he tapped for sugar live from season to season. He was not as mobile as the Indian, but actually did come to settle and preserve his newly found heritage The wooden spout replaced the reed and the wooden bucket the bark trough. Reducing the gathered sap to sugar or syrup was not as easy then as now; the few pieces of bark or other 'woods impurities' seemed all right and did not affect the taste.

"The Potawatomi Indian employed the Maple sap not only as a source of sugar for seasoning but also to yield his vinegar. Some sap was allowed to become sour and made into a vinegar which was used in their preparation of venison, later sweetened with Maple sugar.

"The Indians gather their sugar crop in just the same way as they did many years ago, except that they now use large iron kettles in place of the pottery of former days or in place of the Birch bark vessels before they had pottery. The boiling of sap in Birch bark vessels was quite a difficult thing to do. The flame (of the original fire) must never be allowed to come into contact with the Birch bark but the intense heat of the coals made the sap boil."

The seedlings may be gathered early in April and washed quickly in cold water. In the fresh state they are taken either with a salad, chopped and included in a cole slaw, or steamed with other vegetables. For a soup, they may be used whole or cut but added only near the end of the cooking.

We have collected basketsful of the seedlings every Spring and have dried them for future use.

MARSH MARIGOLD—*Caltha Palustris*

Synonym: Cowslip.

Habitat: Marshes, wet lowlands and meadows.

Part Used: Leaves, flower buds.

Collection: Spring. When gathering the leaves, cut them carefully near the base with a scissors, and thus several crops will be obtained for cooking purposes.

Preparation: The leaves are collected in the Spring and used as a pot herb, prepared and served like Spinach.

The early flower-buds, when pickled in a spiced vinegar, offer an excellent substitute for capers.

Caution: Marsh Marigold should never be eaten uncooked, since in that state, the leaves contain a harmful substance called Helleborin.

The following recipe for creamed Cowslips is reported by Dr. Medsger: "Cook the Cowslip, add pinch of salt, drain well and chop fine. Put a tablespoonful of butter into a saucepan, add a tablespoonful of flour and mix thoroughly. Salt and pepper to taste. Add greens and ½ cup of cream or rich milk. Stir until well mixed and you have an appetizing dish ready to serve."

The farmer's family can feast on Cowslip greens, which city folks rarely see. In our opinion Cowslips are the best of greens. Farmers may not know that the word "Cowslip" is a corruption of "cow's leek." It doesn't taste at all like leeks and we still like what an old Berkshire farmer told us in our youth, that it was called "Cowslip" because it grew in damp meadows and the cows slipped on it.

Here is some advice from *The Whole Body of Cookery Dissected*, written by William Rabisha in 1675.

"To Conserve Cowslips, Marigold, Violets and Scabious: Have the flowers of either of these, being picked clean from those which are withered, and to every ounce of the flowers add three ounces of sugar. First let them be stamped very small without the sugar by themselves. As they grow dry, put them in Rose Water or the juice of lemons, and when they are beaten small enough, put to them your sugar. Beat them together until they are well mingled; after which, you may put them up for use."

Many years ago we transplanted a clump or two of marsh marigolds to the banks of our brook. There they are today covering the banks with gold and spreading into an old alder swamp and on into the damp woods beyond. What a joy they are to our eyes, hungry for color after the long winter. When cowslips are coming into bloom along the brook choose a suitable bowl and a sharp trowel and lift the plant, roots and all. It comes up easily, dripping mud and water, and will fit nicely into the bowl. The blossoms will open in the house and last for along time, and then can go back into the ground none the worse for the experiment.—Ruth D. Grew in *Horticulture*

MASTERWORT—*Heracleum Lanatum*

Synonym: Cow Parsnip.
Habitat: Rich, wet soil.
Part Used: Leaf stalks. Roots. Seeds.
Collection: The young leaves just before the flowers appear; the roots when the herb is 5 or 6 inches high and the seeds before maturing. Dry and store all usable parts for future use.

The young leaves, freshly collected and chopped, may be included in salads of cooked or uncooked vegetables. The early tender roots, whose smell and taste resemble the Parsnip's, are used in soups and stews.

The seeds are collected just before maturing, dried, and used as seasoning for cooked foods, soups, stews, etc.

MILKWEED—*Asclepias Syrica* (L.)

Synonym: Silkweed.

Habitat: Waste areas. Roadsides. Rich composted soils.

Part Used: Early shoots. Pods. Flowers.

Collection: The shoots when 5-6 inches high are most tender in the early morning and are then gathered. The pods, when light green and soft; the flowers when in full bloom. (*Beware of the bees.*)

Preparation: The young shoots are first washed well, and steamed (or cooked) until soft, being prepared like Asparagus. The early pods, alone or with the purple fragrant flowers, may be prepared as fritters or included in soups or stews.

The enterprising herb enthusiast will preserve the tender greens by canning them and will dehydrate and store the early tender pods until needed. Be sure to remove the inner mass of seeds and silk.

The stems in cream sauce may be put into a baking dish, topped with buttered crumbs, and set in the oven until the crumbs are nicely browned.

The Ojibwe Indians, Huron Smith states, use the "flowers and buds in soups. One always finds a riot of Milkweed close to the wigwam or house of the Indians, suggesting that they have been cultivated. Meat soups are thickened with the buds and flowers of the Milkweed and it imparts a very pleasing flavor to the dish." We, too, have found that the flowers do "become somewhat mucilaginous like Okra when cooked."

The flowers were cut up by the Chippewa squaw and stewed, being eaten like preserves. It is said that the herb was sometimes eaten before a feast, so that a man could consume more food.

"It is said that the Indians used the tuberous root of this plant for various maladies, although they could scarcely have known that because of the alleged (?) healing properties of the genus, Linnaeus dedicated it to Aesculapius, of whose name *Asclepias* is a Latinized corruption."

Ascorbic Acid Content per gram of Fresh Weight.
Burdock—0.696 Dandelion—1.546 Milkweed—6.556 Pokeweed—2.735 Watercress—1.875

Note: This Cinderella "weed" has produced food not only in its shoots and pods but in the seeds which contain 20% of edible oil. The seed oil has been found to be similar in quality to Soy Bean Oil. The meal residue following the processing of the seeds is now used for stock feed.

The stalk and silk (floss) of the pods make feather weight clothing, drugs, oils, plastic, insulating board and paper.

"Transplanted from Nature's garden into our own, into what Thoreau termed that 'meagre assemblage of curiosities, that poor apology for Nature and Art which I call my front yard,' clumps of Butterfly weed (*A. Tuberosa*) give the place real splendor and interest," wrote Neltje Blanchan.

One writer has stated that this herb is "worthy of cultivation and is easily transplanted, as the fleshy roots, when broken in pieces, form new plants. Oddly enough, at the Centennial exhibition before the turn of the century, much attention was attracted by a bed of these beautiful plants which were brought over from Holland. Truly, flowers like prophets are not without honor save in their own country."

MOONSEED—*Menispermum Canadense*

The fruits of this shrub are similar in appearance to frost Grapes but are not to be eaten. They are very poisonous and the death of 3 boys, it has been reported, was due to eating them. The action of the toxic ingredient is said to be similar to that of strychnine. Moonseed is related to another poisonous plant, *Cocculus* or Fishberry.

RED MULBERRY—*Morus Rubra* (L.)

Synonym: Common Mulberry.
Habitat: Rich woods.
Part Used: The fruits. When the fruits first ripen, they
    take on a bright red shade, but when fully ripe, their
    color is dark purple.
Collection: When fully mature. July.
Preparation: We have found the freshly expressed juice
    of the ripe, luscious fruits rather cooling and quite
    refreshing as a Summer drink. And when mixed
    with sliced Bananas, fresh Peaches, soured cream
    and cottage cheese, they make a substantial meal
    easily digested and assimilated, replete with blood-
    fortifying minerals and vitamins.

The fruits should enter into pies, jellies, and marmalade preferably made with honey and Lemon and Orange peels.

Mulberry Wine

1. Gather the fruits when red to black, before noon. Allow to dry about 24 hours.
2. Squeeze out the juice and to each gallon of expressed juice, add one gallon of hot water, a few Lemon peels and a little of Cinnamon and Sassafras barks. Slowly bring to a boil and continue the boiling for a half hour.
3. To each gallon, add 6 ounces of sugar and a pint of yellow wine.

4. Allow to stand a week, strain and keep in a cool place.

Rob of Mulberries (An old Arabian Recipe)

Mix 1 pint of the juice of Mulberry fruits with ½ pint of honey. Simmer the mixture until it is reduced to the consistency of clarified honey. (*Rob* is the Arabic word for dense.)

INKY MUSHROOMS—*Coprinus* Species

Clusters of these are usually found growing at the base of dead trees or stumps. These are collected from Spring to Fall, after continued rainy weather.

The Inky Mushroom is so-called because its gills, covered with numerous black spores, dissolve at maturity into an inky fluid.

THE MEADOW PINK or FIELD MUSHROOM—
Psalliota Campestris — *Agaricus Campestris*

"The very common Field Mushroom," wrote W. W. Ray in *Common Edible Mushrooms of Oklahoma*, "is nearly identical in shape, size, color and flavor with the commercially produced mushroom sold in grocery stores. It is found in fields, golf links, pastures and lawns, especially if the ground has been heavily manured. It occurs most frequently from May until July, but it may be gathered throughout the summer and autumn during or following several days of rainy and cloudy weather.

"The cap in the button stage (very young mushrooms) is hemispherical in shape, and as the mushroom matures the cap becomes convex or even flattened. The surface of the cap is normally smooth and presents a soft, silky appearance, but sometimes the cap is covered with brownish scales. The color is usually white, although light-brown forms occur, especially when scales cover the surface. The flesh of this mushroom is white."

MORELS or SPONGE MUSHROOMS—*Morchella*

"All Morels are edible," Ray also wrote, "and are rated among the best mushrooms for eating. They can be dried when cut into small pieces and later used for food after being softened in water.

"The cap is conical to almost spherical and the stems are hollow. Morels make their appearance the first thing in the spring from late March into May. They occur principally in apple orchards, open woods in grassy places and frequently they grow in the grass along the edges of rivers and streams."

OYSTER MUSHROOM—*Pleurotus Ostreatus*

"The Oyster Mushroom," continued Ray, "is frequently encountered growing on logs or dying trees during the months of October through January. Along streams and ditches are the most favorable places to look for it. It is an easy form to recognize, and its flavor and texture are good. Insects do not usually infest this mushroom, and, although it may become frozen, the texture and flavor are not altered.

"In preparation for cooking, one should use the strip of flesh extending inwards from the outer edge about 1 to 2 inches. This is the most tender part, whereas the portion nearest the stem is almost always tough."

PUFF-BALL MUSHROOM—*Calvatia* Species

Dr. Ray states that "all Puff-balls are edible but only when the flesh is soft and white, cheesy in texture and free from insects throughout the entire ball. Small Puff-balls should be cut in two for examination before they are cooked."

When 5 or 6 inches in diameter, they may be peeled and sliced and then baked like Egg-plant.

WILD MUSTARD—*Brassica Arvensis* (L.)

Synonym: Charlock.

Habitat: Quite common in cultivated areas and waste
   places.
Part Used: Leaves.
Collection: Spring.
Preparation: The leaves may be steamed or used either
   in a cold salad or in a soup.

NASTURTIUM—*Trapaeolum Majus*

Synonym: Indian Cress.
Habitat: Cultivated in gardens.
Part Used: Upper half of the plant. Unripened seeds.
Preparation: The common garden Nasturtium provides
   a fair substitute for Watercress, to which it is
   closely related. Both the young leaves and flower
   petals, both eaten always uncooked, produce a most
   palate-teasing effect upon an otherwise dull salad.

The leaves, stems and especially the half-ripened
seeds are often added to a jar containing pickles and
there allowed to remain a few days. They are later mixed
with salad or cole slaw. Pickled Nasturtium seeds are
considered a delicacy by the Chinese.

Pickled Nasturtium Seeds, A Substitute for Capers

1. Gather the seeds as soon as the blossoms are gone.
2. Put them into cold water and salt, and change the
   water for 3 days successively.
3. Prepare a pickle of Nutmeg, Peppercorns, Horseradish and vinegar.
4. Warm but do not boil.
5. Drain the seeds, place in a jar and pour the pickle
   onto them and seal jars.
                          —Modern Domestic Cookery

Saith Pliny: "A sluggish man should eat Nasturtium, to arouse him from his torpidity."

NETTLE—*Urtica Dioica* (L.)

Synonym: Great or Stinging Nettle.

Habitat: Waste places.

Part Used: Young sprouts.

Collection: In Spring, when 6-8 inches high.

Preparation: The Spring greens are best eaten steamed, or cooked but 2 or 3 minutes in the least amount of water; naturally, they may be included in a vegetable soup. They are of antiscorbutic importance, containing a large percentage of Vitamin C, in association with blood-enriching chlorophyll and minerals phosphorus and iron(2.3%) plus a high protein content (5.5%). Any excess should be preserved, either canned or dehydrated.

An entire root section may be forced in one's cellar during the winter months. The quickly growing young shoots, though blanched, may still be used in salad or soup. According to Mr. Kenneth Walker, Health Hobby Club, "No plant is better adapted for forcing; and in winter or spring it may be made to form an excellent substitute for Cabbage or Spinach. Collect the creeping roots and plant them either on a hot-bed or in pots to be placed in the forcing-house, and they will soon send up an abundance of tender tops; these, if desired, may be blanched by covering with other pots."

Of the many references to the edible features of friend Nettle, the following are worthy of attention: In *Les Miserables*, Victor Hugo praises it thus: "One day, he [M. Madeleine] saw some peasants plucking out Nettles and said, 'When the Nettle is young, its leaf forms an excellent vegetable. . . . Chopped, the Nettle is good for poultry, pounded it is good for cattle. . . . The seeds mingled with fodder impart a gloss to animals.' "

Thomas Campbell, the Scottish poet, paid tribute to the herb, saying: "In Scotland, I have eaten Nettles, I have slept in Nettle sheets, and I have dined off a Nettle tablecloth. The young and tender Nettle is an excellent pot herb. The stalks of the old Nettle are as good as flax for making cloth. I have heard my mother say that she thought Nettle cloth more durable than any species of linen."

Samuel Pepys, immortal eavesdropper and diarist, records his visiting the Symons' home in London. Recorded Mr. Pepys: "She like a good lady [was] within and there we did eat some Nettle porridge, which was made on purpose today, and was very good."

"Was it not," asks Charles Francis Saunders in his *Useful Wild Plants of the U. S. and Canada*, "Goldsmith who wrote that a French cook of the olden time could make seven different dishes out of a Nettle-top?"

Organic gardeners should utilize the bounty of the all-important trace minerals and chlorophyll of Nettles. This herb, fully grown, should be carefully gathered, dried and ground finely, and applied as a mulch or organic fertilizer to growing vegetables.

The organic-minded poultry raiser will find that the feed in which ground Nettle leaves have been mixed will insure healthy chickens against diseases and increase their egg production.

The Cursed Weed

Standing on the side of a railroad track, a ragged half starved tramp was vigorously scratching his arm and violently cursing the tall weeds that caused this itching. Usually found growing near the cursed weeds is common Yellow Dock, whose leaves when crushed and applied as poultice offer a soothing relief from the burning itch. The juice of Nettle leaves itself is soothing for the Nettle itch. The miserable tramp did not know this nor did he know that the irritating weed was potentially worth many dollars.

Like the tramp, not much more is generally known about this weed excepting that its common name is Stinging Nettle. Not only is it considered a useless weed but it is hated and often cursed for its rank growth as well as for the stinging hairs that cover the plant.

In Europe there is an entirely different opinion of Stinging Nettle. Folks of the Old World have learned through centuries of experience that Nettle is one of the most useful of all plants.

The young sprouts and tops are used in spring as a pot herb. Boiling renders the stinging hairs harmless. Nettle is a healthy and easily digested vegetable. It is slightly laxative.

In England a pleasant drink known as Nettle Beer is used especially by ailing aged folk. A tea of the dried herb is used medicinally. German soldiers were given mild Nettle Tea with sugar as a substitute for coffee and Oriental tea. The tea was also taken as a 'spring tonic' and beverage during hot weather. An infusion made from the fresh leaves is applied to burns for its soothing effect. . . . —*Meyer's Almanac*

WILD OAT—*Uvularia Perfoliata*

Synonym: Bellwort.
Part Used: Young shoots.
Collection: Spring.

The young shoots may be steamed and served as an Asparagus substitute.

PARTRIDGE BERRY—*Mitchella Repens*

Let us not collect the fruits of this herb for any reason other than to obtain a specimen or two for the herbarium. It is quickly being exterminated by those who search the woods thoroughly for Christmas greenery. The Partridge Berry and the delicate Pipsissewa with its striped leaves are too freely gathered.

"Perhaps that marvelous bird of the woods whose name was given to this plant," warned R.C. Potter, "will not forget the vandalism that took from him his Winter's food. The plant is mountain born and mountain bred. Originating in the slopes of the Andes mountains, where over 100 species occur, it has spread to us, and now faces extinction for its efforts."

PEPPERGRASS—*Lepidium Virginicum*

Synonym: Cress, Land Cress, Bird's Pepper.
Habitat: Dry sandy soil.
Part Used: Leaves. Seed pods.

Collection: The leaves in Spring or early Summer before the herb flowers; the seed pods before ripening. Gather and dry as many of the shoots as space will allow. Their characteristic tang will keep for about two years.

In reference to its rapid growth, it was called Cress, which is derived from the Latin *crescere*, to grow.

The young leaves have a pungent taste, and eaten either alone, mixed into a cole slaw or taken with cold Beet soup, are very good tasting. We enjoy them with diced Cucumber mixed with a mixture of soured cream and cottage cheese.

The seed pods, gathered before ripening in August, may be added as seasoning to a *finished* soup for they (and the leaves) *must not be cooked*. They may also be made into a sauce or dressing, or included in sandwiches.

Peppergrass is an "agreeable vegetable" as the old-timers call it, but especially is it an excellent antiscorbutic which proved to be an invaluable substitute for fresh fruits to the seamen of years ago.

The seeds are relished by birds.

PEPPERMINT—*Mentha Piperita* (L.)

Synonym: American-, Brandy-, Lamb Mint.

Habitat: Waste damp places, marshlands, along brook sides.

Part Used: Dried leaves and flowering tops, collected before the blooming of the flowers. There may be two or more cuttings.

Medicinal uses: Diaphoretic, carminative, nerve stimulant and antispasmodic. Especially useful in colic, dyspepsia, nausea, and general bowel complaints, nervousness and headaches, etc., for which purpose, drink a warm tea of Sage, Skullcap and Peppermint every hour until relieved. To break a cold, try hourly (even half hourly) warm drinks of Peppermint, Elder, Boneset, Sage and Catnip.

As a tisane or carminative: Catnip, Dill and Peppermint (equal parts) may be infused ten minutes and the tea drunk, sipped slowly every ½ hour until relieved. Dose: Teaspoonful of mixed herbs in a cup of hot water, for most stomach ailments.

Peppermint Jelly

1. Simmer for five minutes a handful of washed Peppermint leaves in a glassful of apple or elderberry jelly or commercial jelly. Strain before setting. Add a few drops of green vegetable coloring.
2. Place a handful of ground leaves (tablespoonful each of grated lemon and orange rinds) in two cups of this syrup (1½ cups sugar dissolved in a cup of water), bring to a boil and simmer slowly for twenty minutes. Strain and mix with apple, elderberry or commercial jelly. Other mints that may be substituted—Apple, Bergamot, Curly. (Mrs. Josephine Pierce)

Mint Sauce

A. Quickly prepared, for use with fruits or desserts. Powdered or finely ground leaves are covered with boiling water, and allowed to stand (saucered) until cold—Mix with marmalade.
B. Herb (finely ground) 1 cup; Malt Vinegar, 1 cup; Salt, pinch; Honey, 2 ounces.

The herb is mixed with the vinegar to which the salt has been added; the mixture is simmered ten minutes and allowed to stand covered about 30 minutes. Stir in the honey or enough to thicken to one's taste. Goes well with lamb or chicken.

C. Mix Mint Vinegar with honey.

Mint Vinegar

A. Bring to a boil the vinegar to which is added the sugar and the water-cleansed herb. Stir well and simmer 10 minutes. Strain and immediately pour into hot sterilized bottles.

B.   Pour warmed sugared vinegar onto the herb, cover tightly and let steep two weeks in a warm place. Filter as needed.

Excellent for fruit salads or punch; ingredient of Mint Sauce; or may be used as with the Herb.

C.   Cider Vinegar, 1 pint; Fresh Mint, 1 to 2 cups; sugar, ⅓ to ⅔ cup (optional).

Fruit Cup

With a small scoop make tiny balls of cantaloupe, honeydew melon, watermelon, and add diced fresh pineapple. Put the fruit into a bowl and pour over it a cup of sugar, according to taste, but the mixture should be tart. Add equal proportions of finely chopped leaves of Apple Mint, Orange Mint, Peppermint, about a tablespoon to a quart of fruit. Leave some of the mint to be used later. Let the mixture stand 2 or 3 hours in the ice box. Just before serving, pile the fruit into serving glasses and scatter over the top a bit of mint and a few shavings of candied angelica.

Tisane: Stir well ½ teaspoonful of the dried ground herb in a cup of hot water. Cover 5 minutes, stir and strain. Sip the infusion especially slowly, almost a teaspoonful or so at a time, swished in the mouth before swallowing.

Peppermint tea goes well with the caffeine-bearing Pekoe, for which it should be completely substituted.

Peppermint Tea Leaves

"Peppermint is an age-old health beverage," says Meyer's *Herbalist*, "enjoyed by our grandparents, their parents and many generations before them. Even the aboriginal peoples brewed teas from mints found growing in their native lands. Peppermint tea deserves a come-back because of its real merit as table tea. It deserves a place on the modern table because this high-speed and highly stimulated civilization needs soothing and healthful habits more than ever in the history of the human race. The use of Peppermint tea is so harmless that it can be given to babies with colic (one or two table-spoons of warm Peppermint tea, sweetened with sugar or honey). Peppermint tea may be used alone or made in various ways. Lemon may be added—sweetened if desired or added with other healthful tea herbs such as Alfalfa herb (vitamin rich), Clover flowers (Indian-used tea), Linden flowers (an old European tea)."

PICKEREL WEED—*Pontederia Cordata* (L.)

Synonym: Pike-weed.
Habitat: Borders of muddy ponds and marshes.
Part Used: Fruits.
Collection: When mature.
Preparation: Dried and ground, the fruits containing
the starchy seeds are acceptable as flour substitutes.

It is found in still waters, "of which," said Isaak Walton, "some Pikes [pickerel] are bred." And again we find one E. Moor claiming "that the sun's heat helps the breeding of pike in it."

PIGNUT—*Hicoria Glabra*

If these inch long nuts are supposedly "only fit for pigs," it may also be true that the amount of resultant meal hardly warrants the time gathering them, even more so when other more meaty nuts are available; but that they are "distasteful to human palates" is a statement not wholly justifiable. We have collected our share of the ripe nuts in the fall, taking time to ready the nut-meats for table use while enjoying a Beethoven or Brahms symphony.

Eating the nut recalls memories of my childhood: Good! Sweet!

PIMPERNEL—*Anagallis Arvensis*

Although the ripened seeds have been suggested as a valuable food for song birds, and as a pot herb for humans, it should be considered not as an edible herb but as a medicinal herb. The June-collected herb possesses very active properties and must be handled with care, even when prepared as a tea.

The herb has been used in cases of epilepsy and feverish complaints with reported good results, and more recently in liver and dropsical conditions.

WHITE PINE—*Pinus Strobus* (L.)

Synonym: Weymouth Pine.
Habitat: Rich woods.
Part Used: Inner bark. Leaves (needles). Seeds.
Collection: The bark and leaves in early Spring. The seeds in August, as the cones begin to open.

It may appear incredible to the present day skeptic that, to prevent scurvy, the New England Indians boiled the Spring-collected leaves and drank nothing but the resultant infusion for a week during which time they abstained from solid foods. Several years ago, Dr. Harold Feldman, then of the Massachusetts College of Pharmacy, Boston, investigated the needles of the White Pine and found them to contain a high percentage of Vitamin A. Not only has it recently been shown that certain tree leaves and grassy plants contain considerable amounts of Vitamin C; but Pine needles contain about five times as much Vitamin C as is contained in Lemons, and the Russians have used an infusion of Pine needles as a source of this vitamin.

The Pine bark, coarsely ground or powdered, may be cooked together with Irish Moss and Elm Bark, which see. The seeds may be cooked with meat, as practiced by the Ojibwe. The Indians also used the young staminate catkins and ate them either as a pot herb or stewed with meats.

Note: Adirondack means "tree-eaters."

"During the latter part of the 17th century," wrote Alice Lounsberry, "all silver shillings and smaller coins that were struck in the colony of Massachusetts bore the device of a White Pine."

The *American Botanist* (1910-11 edition) commented upon the value of Pine seeds as a possible source of foodstuffs: "To many in the United States the seeds of the Pine seem to have little economic value. Seeds of the eastern and southern Pines are too small to be of any value, but in the southwest are several species of Pine with seeds large enough to form an appreciable source of food. In some sections Pine seed may be regarded about as beechnuts are in the New England and Middle states, but in others, they are held in high esteem. Gathering Pine seeds is a recognized industry among certain Indian tribes. In South America the Chilian Pine or Monkey-puzzle tree, a plant well known in cultivation in greenhouses on this side of the equator, yields a large amount of food. One tree, it is reported, will supply food for a dozen persons. The cones are 6 inches or more in diameter and each scale encloses 2 seeds an inch or more long. Since the cones are borne in abundance the Pine seed harvest is of much value."

"It was early recognized," adds Richard C. Potter, "by the Indians and the early settlers that the white pine had many medicinal properties as well as food values. The thin layer of delicate and tender tissue just underneath the bark contains a rich descending current of sugary liquid, manufactured by the leaves. There are many instances in the literature of that period as well as in literature of the old world that show that the hungry people were able to sustain life by the gathering of this inner layer of wood with its rich substances of sap and containing a juice as sweet as honey or as sugar. Certainly the drying and eating of the bark with the fat of beasts, sometimes meant the difference between life and death. This was also extended to such trees as the hemlock and the spruce."

PLANTAIN—*Plantago Major* (L.)

Synonym: Cuckoo's Bread.
Habitat: Waste places, gardens and lawns.
Collection: The fruits while still green; the leaves when young and about 2 inches in length.
Preparation: Although Plantain fruits (seeds) are not generally recommended for human consumption, the leaves may be added as an extra to a soup or stew.

The seeds serve well as additional feed for chickens, other domestic fowl, canaries and caged birds, etc. Plantains are not only closely cropped by the herb-hungry poultry; goslings nearing the goose stage delight in gorging themselves on patches of the tough leaves.

WILD PLUM—*Prunus Maritima—Prunus Americanus—Prunus Nigra*

The Beach Plum, *Prunus maritima*, inhabits the sandy rocky areas of our New England coast line and is especially common in Cape Cod. Its fruits are the size and color of Concord Grapes, sweet and juicy, and are of value in the making of preserves, jellies and sauces.

The fruits of the *Americanus* variety are yellow to red color, those of the *Nigra* orange-red and used as above described.

Any excess of fruits should be dried as with Blueberries, Elderberries, et al.

POKE—*Phytolacca Decandra—Phytolacca Americana*

Synonym: Ink Berry, Pigeon Berry, Garget, Pocan.
Habitat: Rich fields. Roadsides.
Part Used: Tender shoots.

Collection: In the Spring, when about 5-6 inches.

Preparation: The first boiling should be quick and no
more than 1 minute and will thus eliminate the prob-
able and needless extraction of nutrients. The
shoots are best steamed for 2 or 3 minutes, may be
cooked in soup, or prepared like Spinach or Asparagus. Yes, do can them.

To cook stalks not over 4 inches long, lay them in
cold water for one hour. Tie loosely in bundles and put
them in boiling water and boil ¾ hour until tender.
Drain and lay them on buttered toast, dust with pepper
and salt, cover with butter and serve.

The Fall roots, transplanted into the cellar and
forced in a box of rich garden soil, will yield a plentiful
supply of blanched shoots.

Poke Greens

"I should like to tell about our way of cooking poke
greens," wrote Rebecca Parker in *Horticulture*. "We add
a handful of young horseradish leaves, if a sprightly flavor is desired. Then we freshen them up in cold water
and cook in rapidly boiling salted water until tender.
Then we drain, add pepper and butter. Serve with vinegar for those who like it."

In praise of Pokeweed: If one wishes to enjoy this salad at
its peak of perfection, the roots should be lifted in the Autumn after
the berries and stalks are dry. Then the roots should be placed in
beds after the fashion of rhubarb and asparagus, being covered
with not less than five inches of mellow soil. This plant will produce large, tender sprouts.

Combine the parboiled leaves with an equal amount of cress,
pepper grass, dandelion or mustard and cook in just enough water
to avoid scorching. When done, add six or eight minced Spring
onions, or their equivalent, which have been sautéed in bacon
drippings or other prepared fat, seasoning to taste. The grated yolk
of hard-boiled egg added just before removing from the heat is
used by some. Garnish with egg rings.—*News Report*

"The vintners in Portugal," Observed Thomas

Green in 1823, "for many years used the juice of these berries to give a deep color to Red Port wines, to which it was thought to communicate a disagreeable taste when mixed in too great a quantity. Complaint of this practice having been made to the government, orders were given that the stems of this plant should be cut down and destroyed before they produced berries.

"English farmers formerly fed their poultry large amounts of these fruits but discovered that although the birds were quite fond of them, the fruits, if eaten in large quantities, would give the flesh a rather disagreeable flavor."

EVENING PRIMROSE—*Oenothera Biennis*

Synonym: German Rampion, Wild Beet, Scurvish, Nightwillow Herb.
Habitat: Waste places. Roadsides.
Part Used: Leaves. Roots.
Collection: The young rosette of leaves and roots of the first year's growth are gathered only in the early Spring.
Preparation: As early as 1614, it was introduced as German Rampion from Europe to America. It was formerly cultivated in English gardens for its edible roots, which were also used as a source of medicine.

The leaves are prepared either as a Spinach or pot herb; the roots cut into small pieces are used in gumbo soup or stews.

The name Wild Beet refers to the beet-like appearance of the thick root of the first year's growth.

PURSLANE—*Portulaca Oleracea*

Synonym: Pussley, Portulaca.
Habitat: Rich garden soil.
Part Used: Herb, minus thick stems.
Collection: Throughout growing season. Dehydrate any excess for future use.

Preparation: Purslane may be prepared for table use in several ways. It is best eaten uncooked, in a salad, and seasoned with olive oil and herb vinegar. Eaten in the Nature-all or uncooked state and included daily in one's Summer or mixed salad, this herb offers far more nutritional value than many garden products.

It may also be steamed or quickly cooked and served like Spinach. Its use as a pot herb has been well-known to the peoples of Europe and Asia. In Mexico, it is a staple item in the open air vegetable marts. Chopped up finely and previously steamed or cooked, it may be baked with other foods, or broiled with fish or meat.

By all means, the conservation-minded householder should preserve Purslane, which in the Winter will be most welcome as a worthy vegetable-substitute. It will be worth the effort to dehydrate as much as your attic will allow.

Remarks: The English diarist John Evelyn tells us to pickle the herb (though only the thick stems should be so processed). Says he: "It is set in vinegar 3 days, reset for another 3 days; boiled 3 hours and set again." (*Ed*. A rather wasteful procedure!)

"I have made a satisfactory dinner on several accounts, simply off a dish of Purslane which I gathered in my cornfield, boiled and salted," wrote Thoreau in *Walden*.

Gerard, the famous herbalist of the 16th century, said of this plant, "Raw purslane is much used in salads, with oil, salt and vinegar. It cools the blood and causes appetite." The same is true today.

"In burning fevers, if chewed, it will cool and refresh. . . . It is eaten with vinegar or else taken with Cummin in drink," wrote Pliny the Elder 1900 years ago.

Several summers ago, the caretaker of Tuck Farm, Auburn, Mass., asked me to identify a plant which had spread quite profusely over a portion of his vegetable area. Here and there were huge piles of the herb discarded as worthless, ready to be carted away and dumped. My friend, the caretaker, was most pleasantly surprised when I advised him to either make use of this edible as previously described or by all means to apply the discards as a much needed mulch to his many rows of hungry vegetables. Conservation, to him, now means providing better produce and saving money via the eating of "weeds."

If you are fortunate enough to know any gardener who wants to get rid of any Pussley, by all means transplant a few plants in an area which will permit the free spreading of this worthwhile vegetable. Be sure that you obtain as much of the root system as possible. Moreover, should you discover any Pussley plants that have already gone to seed, remove and dry the seeds for several days. Then sow in fairly good soil and in 6 to 7 weeks a new crop has about matured and is fit to eat, but be sure to water the young plants in dry weather at least twice a week. To have a steady succession of crops, cut the plants near the base and more fresh will grow.

RAGWEED—*Ambrosia Artemisiaefolia* (L.)

The flower heads are dried and fed to caged birds.

Although Ragweed is the bane of hay-fever sufferers, out in Michigan they say that it is the staff of life to pheasants in Winter, when practically all food for pheasants has disappeared. Ragweed is excellent sheep food and I have seen large stacks of it put up for the Winter. Further, it now appears that this plant, or its seed, yields a valuable oil, and I understand that considerable crops of this seed have been harvested in Indiana. . . . And in all fairness to the pro-Ragweeders, it must be stated that it has been determined that Ragweed seeds do contain an extractable oil resembling that obtained from Soybean.

RASPBERRY—*Rubus* Species

Habitat: Waste places. Borders of woods.
Part Used: Fruits and leaves.
Collection: Mid-Summer, when fruits have matured.
Preparation: The fruits, though generally used in the
    preparation of home-made jams and jellies, should
    be eaten uncooked whenever possible, if one is to
    benefit from all of the nutritive values of this ubi-
    quitous native. Any excess should be dehydrated
    and saved for future use. They may also be in-
    cluded in the manufacture of an herb wine.

The dried early leaves serve well as a tea substitute,
when mixed with Mint, dried Lemon and/or Orange
peels.

The New England Farmer says that, "Raspberries
may be preserved wet, bottled, or made jam or marmalade of, the same as strawberries. Raspberries are very
good dried in the sun or in a warm oven. They are very
delicious stewed for table or tarts."

Dr. William Meyrick had high praise for the fruits
and urged his patients to eat much of them, fresh and
cooked. Said he, "The juice of the ripe fruit boiled into a
syrup, with sugar, is pleasant and agreeable to the
stomach, and prevents sickness and reachings." And Dr.
Withering, the first physician to prescribe Digitalis,
also recommended it: "The fruit is very grateful as nature presents it, but made into a sweet-meat with sugar,
or fermented in wine, the flavour is greatly improved. It
is fragrant, a little acid, and of a cooling nature. It dis-
solves the tartareous concretions on the teeth, but is in-
ferior to strawberries for that purpose."

Here are two recipes from the *New England Farmer*.

Raspberry Jam

"Weigh the fruit, and add three-quarters of the

weight of sugar; put the former into a preserving pan, boil, and break it; stir constantly, and let it boil very quickly; when the juice has boiled an hour, add the sugar and simmer half an hour. In this way the jam is superior in color and flavor to that which is made by putting the sugar in at first."

Raspberry Wine

"Bruise the finest ripe raspberries with the back of a spoon; strain them through a flannel bag into a stone jar; allow one pound of fine-powdered loaf sugar to one quart of juice; stir these well together, and cover the jar closely; let it stand three days, stirring the mixture up every day; then pour off the clear liquid, and put two quarts of sherry to each quart of juice, or liquid. Bottle it off, and it will be fit for use in a fortnight."

WILD RICE—*Zizania Palustris* (L.)—*Zizania Aquatica* (L.)

Synonym: Water Oats, Indian Rice.
Habitat: Still ponds.
Part Used: The seeds.
Collection: Late Summer.

The joyous occupation of harvesting and preserving Wild Rice was so important to several of the Indian tribes that, according to Melvin Gilmore, in his *Indian Lore and Indian Gardens*, the month in which it ripens was named for it. And the name of one of these tribes, (a member) of the Algonquin stock called the Menomini, derives its name from the word for Wild Rice, namely Manomin; so the Menomini are the Manomin people or the Wild Rice people."

When Jacques Cartier of St. Malo, Normandy, reported his trip in 1534 for King Francis I of France, he called it "a kind of wild corn, like unto rye."

Huron Smith, who was recognized as the foremost authority on the Midwest Indians, stated that "the slight-

ly burned taste that stays with the (wild) rice (previously parched but not scorched, to destroy any eggs of insects which might be in the rice), is highly relished by
the Indians and perhaps as much so by the white people.
Wild Rice increases in size from 3-4 times during the
process of cooking. Often times they make what would
correspond to a pudding from Wild Rice and sweeten
this with Maple sugar. . . . It has been said that there
is as much nutriment in a bushel of Wild Rice as there is
in a bushel of Wheat and this is doubtless so. The Wild
Rice grains are about 3 times the size of wheat grains
and while they are dark brown or black on the outside,
when they are cooked they are white inside."

Professor Medsger has testified that Wild Rice is
"pleasant eating," stating that "we have cooked it in the
same manner as cultivated Rice and served it warm with
butter and salt to season, or cold with sugar and cream."

Wild Rice was the principal cereal food among
many of the Indians and was cooked alone and also with
meat or game. The parched seeds were boiled in water
or in animal fat and seasoned with Maple syrup. And to
this mixture, dried Blueberries were often added. With
Blueberries, the freshly collected Rice was stored and
dried and cooked during the Winter months and Spring.
It is interesting to note that among the Chippewa, the
chaff from the treading (preparation) of the Rice was
cooked similarly to the Rice and was considered a delicacy.

WILD ROSE—*Rosa Canina* (L.)

Synonym: Dog Rose, Brier Rose.
Habitat: Gravelly soil. Roadsides.
Part Used: Ripe fruits (hips). Petals. Leaves.
Collection: Fruits in September, when fully colored. The
    petals and leaves, mid-Summer.
Preparation: The dried petals and leaves are often used
    with Peppermint, Lemon peel, and Linden leaves

as a tea substitute, especially adapted for folks with arthritis or dyspepsia, and for others who cannot tolerate the excessive tannic acid of tea or coffee or who do not wish to ingest the heart-stimulating caffeine of those beverages. Rose petals contain malic and tartaric acids and are said to be of great value in "dissolving out" gallstones and gravel from the urinary organs.

However, the hips, as the fruits are commonly called, have recently come into prominence as a superior natural source of Vitamin C, possessing 60 times that of Lemons. Appreciable quantities of citric and malic acids and natural sugar are also present. Each small fruit is reported to yield 10 mg. of Vitamin C. And, too, British scientists have also found that these fruits are good sources of Vitamins A and P. The latter is present in the peel of most citrus fruits, plays an important role in the prevention of rupture and bleeding of the minute capillary vessels, and aids the healing of wounds.

As reported in *The American Botanist*, the fruit of the Wild Rose formed the principal sustenance of the Doukhobors, or Spirit Wrestlers, of Western Canada, upon their 10 days' religious pilgrimage across the prairies.

During World War II when there were not enough Oranges in Britain for children, Rose hips were processed to yield a syrup of Vitamin C, 2 teaspoonfuls a day giving all of that vitamin required by older children. Wild Rose fruit jam was found by Irish scientists to be particularly acceptable to the digestive systems of infants.

One British scientist in a news story explains how in 1940 the English overcame the shortage of Vitamin C foods: "We found another source of Vitamin C in Rose hips—the red fruit left after a Wild Rose grows in hedges. So we set the children and teachers in the country to collecting them. Everybody else who took a week-end walk in the country carried a basket to gather Rose hips, and turned them in. There was a big basket in the Ministry of Health where we all dumped our contributions Monday morning."

According to the *Journal of the Canadian Medical Association*, it is claimed that the Vitamin C extract from the fruits of the Wild Rose crop in Alberta alone would be more than 10 times the amount necessary for a generous yearly ration of the all-important vitamin for the entire population of Canada.

The herbalists of the Elizabethan era also praised the edible virtues of Rose, wild and cultivated, to wit: "The Rose doth deserve the prime place among all floures whatsoever, being not only esteemed for his beauty, vertues, and his fragrant and odoriferous smell.

"The destilled water of Roses is good for the strengthening of the heart, and refreshening of the spirits and likewise for all things that require a gentle cooling. The same being put in junketting dishes, cakes, sauces, and delectable taste.

"Of like vertues also are the leaves of these preserved in Sugar, especially if they be only bruised with the hands, and diligently tempered with sugar, and so heat at the fire rather than boyled."

Processing Rose Hips

The processing of Rose hips or fruits rich in Vitamin C is clearly stated in the *Agricultural Gazette* of New South Wales. To make Rose hip puree use the following method: Select two pounds of Rose hips (either red or orange) and ready two pints of water. Wash the berries well, remove the withered flower ends, and place in a saucepan with the water. Boil till tender (about 20 minutes) and rub through a sieve. Use as required.

Rose Hip Jam

"To make Rose Hip jam take two pints of Rose Hip

puree, four apples and two and one-half pounds of sugar. Proceed as follows:

1. Wash and peel the apples, cut into quarters and core.
2. Stew the apples until tender with just enough water to cover.
3. When the apples are tender, add the rose hip puree and sugar.
4. Heat gently until the sugar is dissolved, then boil until skin forms on the surface of a test sample poured onto a cold plate.
5. Pour into hot sterilized jars and seal immediately.
6. Store in a cool, dark place.

Care must be taken that the jam is thoroughly cooked to evaporate excess moisture. It is best to cook the fruit very thoroughly before adding the sugar, and the time of cooking after the sugar is added should be the shortest possible."

This recipe is from *Horticulture*.

Rose Hip Soup

In Sweden, rose hip soup is a popular, healthful dish. It's easy to make: The hips are ground and boiled for 10 minutes, then strained and again brought to a boil and thickened with 4 level teaspoons of potato flour (you can use soybean or whole wheat flour) which has been prepared with two cups of cold water. This soup can be served hot or cold.

"No matter how you get your rose hips, you can be sure you're treating yourself to one of nature's greatest treasures of nutrition," says *Prevention*.

Rose Hip Syrup

Gather 2 lbs. rose hips, ripe and red. Wash and place in a pan. Cover well with water and bring to a boil. Simmer until tender, about ten minutes. Mash thoroughly with a wooden spoon. Put in flannel jelly bag and squeeze out as much juice as possible. Return pulp to pan and add the same amount of water as before. Bring to a boil and simmer for 5-10 minutes. Put back into jelly bag and squeeze again. Empty bag and wash it thoroughly. Mix the two lots of juice and pour into the clean bag. Let it drip overnight. A clean juice is thus obtained.

The juice may be heated to boiling and poured into sterile jars, sealed and stored indefinitely.

This recipe requires no sugar. To sweeten, add a *little* sugar or honey when serving the concentrate.

Rose Hip Jam

Remove the seeds from very ripe rose hips, sprinkle the flesh with fresh water to which may be added a small glass of wine. Let them stand in a cool place for three to four days, stirring occasionally. Run them through fine sieve. Heat together 2½ cups pulp and 2 scant cups of sugar, stirring until thick.

Note: When you prepare any of these recipes do not use aluminum or copper utensils; the latter destroys the Vitamin C content on contact while the former causes considerable loss, says *Prevention*.

Prevention tells us that we are to follow these rules regardless of what we are making.

"1. Trim both ends of the Rose hips with a pair of scissors before cooking. 2. Use stainless steel knives, wooden spoons, earthenware or china bowls, and glass or enamel saucepans. 3. Cook quickly with the lid on so there will not be much loss of Vitamin C. 4. After the hips have been cooked the required time, strain out the spines and seeds, or break them down by rubbing the cooked pulp through a sieve."

WILD SARSAPARILLA—*Aralia Nudicalis*

Synonym: False Spikenard, Wild Licorice.

Habitat: Rich, moist and shaded woods.
Part Used: The root system.
Collection: Fall.

The long creeping, fragrant root possesses therapeutic properties similar to those of the True Honduras species, as a "blood purifier," anti-rheumatic and diaphoretic. It is often recorded as an old Indian remedy to promote the removal of blood toxins during pregnancy and to insure painless childbirth.

In recent years the root has gained deserved prominence as an ingredient of herb or root beers, and when home-made, such a preparation will be zestful, healthful, and far more enjoyable than store-bought beverages. Grandfather's recipe for his well known Spring (Blood) Tonic was a beer low in alcoholic content (just enough to serve as a preservative) but high in the much-needed components of such worthies as Sarsaparilla, Burdock and Dandelion roots, Sassafras bark and Red Clover. The amounts? A handful of this herb and that herb, though generally an equal amount (more or less) of each ingredient was used.

SASSAFRAS—*Sassafras Albidum—Sassafras Variifolium*

Synonym: Wild Cinnamon, Mitten Plant.
Habitat: Rich woods.
Part Used: Leaves. Bark.
Collection: Leaves intended as a pot herb should be tender and gathered in Spring, in the early morning. The bark is a Fall product.
Preparation: Sassafras is a shrub, 8 to 15 feet high, or a small tree, 20 to 40 feet high, quite common in New England, and is usually called the "mitten plant" since one of its three kinds of leaves growing on the same tree is shaped like a mitten. The name Sassafras is a corruption of the Spanish word *Saxifrage*, which in turn is derived from two Latin

words, *saxum*, meaning "a rock," and *frango*, meaning "I break." It is interesting to note that herbalists recommend to those sufferers with stones in the kidneys and other kidney diseases that Sassafras be always included in a formula of kidney-stimulating herbs. Other medicinal uses of Sassafras shrub include employing its spongy pith in combination with Witch Hazel leaves, as a very efficient eye lotion, while the bark and roots are included in a "blood purifying" formula.

The leaves, twigs and berries all have a characteristic spicy odor and taste, though I prefer the bark and berries for seasoning, the early leaves for soup. Years ago, my mother often prepared for us youngsters what she called "country soup" into which went such well knowns as young Burdock stems and wild Goosefoot, Peppergrass, Dandelion, and of course, Sassafras leaves, which helped to thicken and give the soup that certain extra bit of "oomph"— or, as Poet Clinton Scollard has so aptly written:
"When the Sassafras you bruise
There's a perfume fit to fill a cruse."
Should you come across a cookbook of Southern recipes, invariably you will find a soup recipe called Creole or Gumbo filé which is a favorite down South, especially in Louisiana and Florida. (And the Choctaw Indians had taught the Whites the various culinary uses of this all-purpose herb.) In this recipe, fragrant Sassafras leaves play an important role, and finely ground or powdered, are added for their pleasant aroma, as well as the required thickening of the soup.

Frank R. Arnold reports in *Horticulture* that "only in Louisiana has Sassafras come into its own, for there it is used in soups under the name of gumbo filé. This is the powdered dried leaves of Sassafras. They have a sweet fragrance, a sort of soapy perfume, and increase the mucilaginous effect of the gumbo in soup. The Creole filé has remained the same as it was in primitive Indian times, simply the Sassafras leaves dried, powdered and put through a sieve, sometimes with the addition of a few wild bay leaves to increase the flavor."

Many herb enthusiasts have reported to me their profitable experiences with using the leaves in chicken Gumbo and other soups, stews, etc. To wit: "Found some interesting soups more desirable, palatable (for a diabetic)." "Used it (the powder) in a salt shaker for table use, instead of and like salt and pepper." "Encouraged my using more of Nature's own (wild growing) foods and seasonings." "Am now making better use of the three Sassafras trees on my property."

In London about a hundred years ago, it was the custom for all chimney sweeps, usually youngsters of 12-15, to partake of several cups of warm Sassafras tea before, during and after working hours. This drink was known as Salop (or Saloop), a corrupted form of the "Sahlep" of Turkey and the Near East countries where it originated as a nutritious beverage. (Sahlep was prepared by dissolving the powdered extract of certain species of Orchids in hot water and adding to this solution a little sugar and milk.) One may well imagine the express delight of the chimney sweep as he sipped his Salop of Sassafras and was almost immediately benefited by the demulcent and antiseptic properties of the herb, as the solution soothed, cleansed, and protected the inflamed or irritated mucous membranes of the throat from future diseases.

Charles Lamb reported the drink as being sold at the "Salopian Shop" on London's Fleet Street and describes it as a "composition, of which I have understood to be the sweet wood yclept Sassafras. This root boiled down to a kind of tea, and tempered with an infusion of milk and sugar, hath to some tastes a delicacy beyond the China luxury." However, Mr. Lamb does confess his

lack of interest in the concern of Sassafras tea, with this
remark: "For myself. . . . I have never yet adventured
my own particular lip in a basin of his commended ingredients— a cautious premonition to the olfactories
constantly whispering to me, that my stomach must in-
fallibly, with all due courtesy, decline it."

And so, too, would many an herb enthusiast decline
a "boiled" tea of the root (bark) as above described by
Author Lamb. To prepare a cup of herb tea, *never boil*
the herbs in the water; do stir a half teaspoonful of the
ground bark in a cup of boiling water and cover with a
saucer for about five minutes. Stir, strain and add a
little honey to sweeten. Sassafras tea has for centuries
been employed as a "blood purifer" and "spring tonic" to
thin out the blood in the Spring. "Sassafras tea," says the
herbalist, slightly prejudiced, "Nectar of the Gods!"

A letter sent by Dr. E. L. Lee of Bridgeport, Alabama, in 1907 to the *American Botanist* said in part:
"We were a little amused by the statement in a recent
number, that Sassafras teas were used during the Civil
War by the people of the South. So it was, but it was used
from choice and a taste long cultivated. Long before the
war, both Whites and Indians made Sassafras tea during
the spring when the sap of the Sugar maples was running. They boiled the sap a while, then added the Sassafras roots and boiled them a while longer and the tea was
finished, and a drink fit for the gods was the result. Was
this fact alone not the cause of drinking Sassafras tea in
the spring of the year?"

To put Sassafras leaves and bark to further use,
combine the leaves with those of Sweet Fern for fragrant
herb pillows; the powdered bark is a good ant powder.

If one has ever chewed a tasty Sassafras twig or
leaf or sipped a bit of the savory sap, one certainly may
sense a feeling of nostalgia and agree with Julia E.
Rogers when she says in *The Tree Book*: "Who has not

nibbled the dainty green buds of Sassafras in winter, or dug at the roots for a bit of their aromatic bark? Or who has not searched among the leaves for mittens? Surely there are people whose youth was spent in regions that knew not this little tree of the fence corners and woodland borders, and they have missed something very much worthwhile out of their childhood."

Perhaps no tree in this country has had a more interesting career than the Sassafras. The American Indian knew that the brew made from its bark was effective in relieving certain ailments. The early explorers, troubled with scurvy, were told by the Indians to use this brew. It worked so well the explorers on their return to Europe spread the news.

The bark and wood have a pleasant taste and it is not to be wondered that the Indians made use of them as well as the leaves, which were often used as a substitute for meat. Soon it became an article of commerce as the seedlings grew. At one time in the illustrious career of Sir Walter Raleigh, he had a monopoly of trade in Sassafras bark, wood and extracts, which undoubtedly netted him a substantial monetary return. He made it a necessity, since its use was claimed to cure a tremendous variety of ailments, in every medicine cabinet in Europe. In later years, its use was nearly universal as a Spring tonic, somewhat akin to the use in our day of sulphur and molasses.

Thus Sassafras has had an intensely medicinal history. It has been variously a panacea for nearly all ills, a dye, a tea, a perfume, a condiment, a drink and finally a flavor. But there are still those who hold that its most potent use is that of a Spring tonic. Sassafras, after playing an important role in American history as the first cartel, enjoys today a quiet reputation as a cherished Spring-time beverage. But its use in providing for children an experience in collecting mittens will remain as its chief claim to fame.

—*Richard C. Potter*

Folks need something warm to drink while they're not drinking dollar coffee and my suggestion is that they drop out to the woods almost anywhere and chop off a few Sassafras shoots. When boiled a while these make a brew that doesn't taste like coffee, according to my friend, Joe E. Johnston of Mt. Pleasant, Tenn. He says it tastes better. Now that I have sampled his formula, I wouldn't argue with him.

He sent me parcel post a big chunk of Sassafras root, carefully wrapped. Seeping through the cracks in the package was an aroma so pleasantly spicy that the post office at McLean, Va., took on a magnificent new smell. This odor now has been transferred to my bride's kitchen and there magnified. There's nothing like boiling Sassafras root to make a house smell nice.

Donor Johnston included directions. He said whack off a chunk of root with a hatchet, toss it in a pot of water and let it simmer a while. Then pour yourself a cup of ambrosial liquid, stir in a little sugar and maybe a dollop of cream, and be glad you're living. This I have tested, with results as predicted, and costly coffee means nothing much to me. The beauty about Sassafras root is that it doesn't perform like a tea bag.

The same piece of Sassafras can be boiled and boiled once more, time and time again, without losing its flavor. Since it costs nothing in the first place, this added economy makes it impossible for coffee at any price to compete.

Still and all the naturalist and philosopher, Thoreau, who spent a Winter by the pond, said Sassafras is easy to recognize. Its leaves look like those of mountain laurel and when you crush them in your hand, according to Mr. T., they give off a heavenly odor of lemon blossoms.—*News Column*

SCURVY GRASS—*Cochlearia Officinalis* (L.)

Habitat: Sea coast, and mountainous wet areas.
Part Used: The leaves.
Collection: Whenever available.

Scurvy Grass is a member of the anti-scurvy Cruciferae family which includes such well-knowns as Watercress, Radish, Cauliflower, Kale, Cabbage and Peppergrass. The bright green, dried leaves of this highly antiscorbutic herb were prepared into infusions by seafaring men of the early 1800's as a far more easily obtainable substitute for Lemons. Thus we learn that wherever around the world he traveled, Captain James Cook advertised the wondrous effect of this scurvy-preventing herb, and as a result, many others anticipating a long sea voyage, had much of it gathered, dried and baled. Scurvy Grass was indeed the chief plant available in large quantities to combat the disastrous scourge of seafaring men.

Its taste is not unlike Watercress, for which it

should be substituted whenever possible. For best results eat the herb in a salad, fresh and uncooked. Heat will cause a great loss of the Vitamin C content.

We learn from *Clinical Excerpts* (Vol. 16, No. 4) that "After a long hard campaign the legions of Rome crossed the Rhine into what is now northern Holland, but due to the exigencies of the war, scurvy became rife among them. Fortunately for the invaders the Frieslanders were able to show them how to cure their malady with certain antiscorbutic herbs, probably scurvy grass, which has long been employed in the Netherlands as a household remedy against the ailment since earliest times. In the sixteenth century a Dutch physician, Forestus of Delft, learned of the remedy from the country folk and concocted a syrup from the herb and from *Veronica beccabunga* (*European Speedwell*), which he sold throughout Flanders and Brabant as an antiscorbutic, thereby gaining a considerable reputation."

SEAWEED (see Irish Moss)

LAVER—*Poryphyra Vulgaris*

A sort of condiment may be prepared by cooking the leaves of the seaweed with Lemon juice. It may be used, cut into inch pieces, in soups and stews. The Chinese make cakes of it, by drying and then simmering it like Irish Moss, to obtain a nutritious jelly.

DULSE—*Rhodymenia Palmata*

This is one of the purplish-red algae, much of which is collected along the shores of New England. It is dried and packed for sale. It is used as a pudding thickener and as a source of iodine. We have often eaten dried Dulse as a nibble (or substitute for candy) although others, who have objected to its unconventional natural taste and appearance, dip bits of it in jelly.

"Culinary advice about Dulse varies," wrote Ethel

Wilson in *Nature*: "Some suggest that it should be put in a pan and fried as soon as picked. Others put it on the stove and let it frizzle up, finding it then ready to chew. One old lady said, 'Dip it in vinegar and then eat it.' Another recommendation was that it should be eaten along with a piece of molasses candy. Children start to chew it at about 4 years, and seem to love its fishy, salty flavor."

KELP

Various Seaweeds, including the *Alaria* and *Fucus* species, have been used as a source of food and medicine. Moreover, its ever-present availability along the coast and its high content of minerals should encourage the farmers along the coastline to gather and use much of this material as a valuable green manure and fertilizer. As a source of potash, says one authority, fresh Kelp produces 20-40 pounds per ton, and dried, 60-200, and its use should be therefore highly encouraged.

In France, powdered, dried Kelp is fed to horses as a matter of course, given plain or mixed with the usual fodder; and it is always fed to sick or ailing horses.

Another species of Seaweed has been used as a source of "supplementary minerals," and its powder manufactured into compressed tablets, sold commercially as Iodine Ration Tablets.

Seaweed Agar Plant Slated

Proposed construction of a $75,000 plant near Apalachicola, Florida, for the manufacture of agar from seaweed was announced today by Arthur L. Tucker, Jr., president and manager of Florida Agar Products, Inc. Agar is a gelatinous substance used as a jelling agent and bacteriological culture.—*News Report*

Algae May Provide Food

In years to come food may be quite different from the kind you're accustomed to eating now. An agricultural scientist says algae, microscopic green plants found in water, may be one source of food in the future.

Algae reproduce much faster than conventional crops. One pound of a common form of algae contains protein equivalent to that in two pork chops, fat equal to that in a fourth of a pound of butter, and carbohydrate equal to that in a heaping tablespoon of sugar.—*News Report*

SHADBUSH—*Amelanchier Canadensis*

Synonym: Juneberry, Serviceberry.
Habitat: Gravelly soil and wet hillsides, banks of streams.
Part Used: Fruits.
Collection: Late June to August. Look for a small tree whose fruit-bearing limbs, advises one authority, may be bent to the ground without breaking, the easier to gather the ripe, red-purplish fruits.

The Indians called this shrub the Serviceberry since they made great use of the fruits, which they gathered in large quantities to be "crushed and pounded and utilized in a sort of cake." However, to the Chippewa, the fruits meant more than having these as a delicacy, often preferring them to Blueberries, for to them this was the Juneberry: "Take some Juneberries with you," was a common saying among them. A certain song, we are told, contains the words: "Juneberries I would take to eat on my journey if I were a son-in-law."

The name Juneberry signifies the time (late June) when the seedy fruits begin to mature, for then they are of a reddish hue later ripening to a full dark purple; and Shadbush refers to the shrub's blossoming when the shad begin to swim up the stream to spawn.

To enjoy the fruits and their sweet, pleasant odor and taste, serve them as dessert, uncooked, with other fresh fruits. They have been used as added ingredients for pies, and preserved and canned for Winter use. And too, they may be used with Elder fruits in wine making.

SHEEPBERRY—*Viburnum Lentago*

Synonym: Wild Raisins, Nannyberry.
Habitat: Edges of rich, moist woods and streams.
Part Used: The fruits.
Collection: Late Summer to Fall. The dark purple fruits may be gathered even during the Winter months, being not harmed at all by the frost; best of all they cure and dry themselves on the tree.

Writing in *Nature Magazine*, Dr. Stephen F. Hamblin stated: "The larger birds eat them and the Indians considered them a useful winter fruit. They are decidedly edible, especially as a relish in the middle of a winter's hike, with a flavor quite like raisins, or the humble but wholesome prune. When cooked, except for the smaller stone, they quite resemble the favored (not favorite) morning-cooked fruit of the boarding-house table, for it is rich in sugar and iron. This is a strictly American fruit whose story is told in the words, 'It might have been.' Had raisin and prune not been brought over by our forefathers, our plant breeders could have taken this shrub and improved the size and flavor of the fruit, perhaps to outrank the prune."

SHEEP SORREL—*Rumex Acetosella* (L.)

Synonym: Sour Grass. (Acetosella—Little Vinegar Plant)
Habitat: Sandy soil.
Part Used: Fresh leaves.
Collection: Whenever available.
Preparation: This is something different for that thick soup or puree, cold salads, and cole slaw.

Sheep's Sorrel is related to and is a miniature form of the Garden Sorrel (*Rumex acetosa*) and like the latter is highly acid in taste and reaction. This very acidity, which is due to the potassium and tartaric acid plus the plant's content of Vitamin C, makes it an important salad green. It should be used as a cooling drink in feverish conditions.

Farm folk consider Sheep Sorrel a good indicator of sour soil.

This plant is *not* related to Wood Sorrel, *Oxalis acetosella* (Synonym: Trefoil, Shamrock) though one may be substituted for the other as an edible or culinary herb.

Sorrel Soup

Wash Sorrel and put in a saucepan with a little water (not covered). Cook slowly for about ½ hour. Put four cups of milk with white onion (whole) in double boiler, add two tablespoonsful of butter plus two of flour to the hot milk. Let stand and add Sorrel and strain. Season to taste.

SHEPHERD'S PURSE—*Capsella Bursa-pastoris* (L.)

Synonym: Lady's Purse, Pepper and Salt.
Habitat: Sandy, waste places.
Part Used: Leaves, fruits.
Collection: The leaves, before the herb flowers. The fruits, before complete maturity.
Preparation: An important vegetable herb found growing wild in gravelly or sandy soil is Shepherd's Purse. It is another example of useful plants just pleading not to be ignored, but to be gathered by all passersby and used as medicine and/or food.

Its antiscorbutic, stimulant and diuretic action caused it to be much used in kidney complaints and dropsy. I am sure that you will enjoy the peppery flavor of the green leaves of the Shepherd's Purse in cole slaw, and for this reason, it is called "salt and pepper" by some farmfolk.

As this herb matures, it produces flat seed-pouches which resemble an old-fashioned change purse, hence its familiar name. Be sure to collect such plants, and when they are completely dry, strip the leaves and small fruit pods and preserve in sterilized, dry glass jars. These come in handy later in the fall and winter, and combined with Peppergrass, add new zip and zest to one's usual vegetable soup.

A mixture of the seeds of Shepherd's Purse and Wild Goosefoot is a valuable food for most caged birds.

One authority suggests that the seeds should be cultivated in the garden and the resultant leaves will be as succulent as the nature and state of the soil where the plants grow. (*Ed*: We are interested in obtaining the optimum values of plant nutrients and these are found only in such herbs as grow in their original natural habitat.)

SILVERWEED—*Potentilla Anserina* (L.)

Synonym: Goose Tansy.
Habitat: Clayey and wet places. We have found them
    growing along sandy roadsides.
Part Used: The roots.
Collection: Spring.

When freshly collected, this root resembles Parsnip in taste. To best enjoy the benefits of this root vegetable, collect it preferably in the morning, wash and refrigerate it until needed but not longer than 5 hours, then steam it 3-4 minutes in a little hot water.

Thomas Green quotes one Ray who had earlier observed that in Yorkshire, England, the roots were called Moors, and during the winter the boys dug them up and ate them. He adds that he was a witness to swine devouring them greedily, and that an apothecary in that neighborhood assured him that they had a sweet taste like Parsnips. The common people in Scotland frequently eat them roasted or boiled. "In the islands of Tyrie and Col, they are much esteemed as answering in some measure the purposes of bread, and have been known to support the inhabitants for months together during a scarcity of other provisions. In their barren and impoverished soils, and in seasons wherein their crops succeed the worst, the roots of the Moors never fail to afford a reasonable relief."

SKUNK CABBAGE

Synonym: Wild-Cabbage, Meadow Cabbage, Skunk-
  weed.
Habitat: Swamps, wet lowlands.
Part Used: Leaves, roots.
Collection: Both in the Spring, the roots 2-3 weeks following the leaves.
Preparation: The early leaves must be washed well,
  twice with cold water. Be sure to discard the water
  of the first cooking. They may be prepared as a
  Spinach, cooked as a Cabbage substitute, though
  for a maximum nutriment the leaves should be
  quickly steamed or pressure cooked only 1 or 2
  minutes. Season to your taste. In either case, dairy
  products as cheese, clabber or soured cream should
  accompany this food to offset the presence of oxalates, which are present also in Sorrel and Cranberries. (The presence of excessive oxalates in Rhubarb forbids the eating of that food.) Yes, do dehydrate the leaves and preserve in sterilized, dry
  jars.

A nourishing flour may be made from the washed roots which, when allowed to dry at least 5 to 6 weeks and then are finely powdered and sifted, are used as described under Jack--in-the-Pulpit.

The roots may be forced in the cellar. The whole

root system is dug up carefully on a rainy day or following rain, and packed with leaf mold and rich loam.

Some of the more argumentative and attentive listeners to my radio broadcasts have raised certain ques-
tions concerning my talk on Skunk Cabbage. I had said,
"Have you ever eaten Wild or Skunk Cabbage? In spite
of your smiles and doubts, young Skunk Cabbage leaves
are not as malodorous as they may sound. Prepared in a
waterless or steam cooker and seasoned with Caraway
seeds, this vegetable proves to be as edible and nutritious
as garden Cabbage."

As a result, I was nearly deluged by a storm of letters protesting against such a statement, and some letters
stated, "Remember Skunk Cabbage is poisonous". . . .
"You ought to be ashamed of yourself for encouraging
such a thing.". . . . "What are you trying to do—poison
us?" . . . . "You speak of Skunk Cabbage as if it could
be preserved and even marketed for sale to the consumer
like any other canned vegetable," etc.

If a dish of steamed Skunk Cabbage, or Wild Cabbage, as I would rather call it, were placed before the
skeptic without his knowing that it was Skunk Cabbage,
I'll wager that he'd ask for a second helping. As for its
being preserved, my method is dehydration. The young
leaves are dried thoroughly, ground as finely as desired
and preserved in a clean and sterilized dry jar.

As for its being marketed, well—that's not such a
bad idea. In fact, I have mentioned in previous broadcasts, as far back as 1941, that people would soon see to
their amazement such items on the market as powdered
green grass and Alfalfa. Several years later, I was able to
corroborate my statements with proof of grass products
which I had displayed on exhibition at the Museum of
Natural History, together with specimens of store Dandelion and Chicory leaves, and our friend Skunk Cabbage.
Moreover, the nutritive factors of this much maligned

swamp-dweller are nothing to sneeze at, as it were; it contains organic fat, starch and oils, and easily assimilated salts of calcium, silica, iron and manganese.

As for the medicinal virtues of Wild Cabbage, Professor Heber W. Youngken, of the Massachusetts College of Pharmacy, declares in his *Textbook of Pharmacognosy* that the roots are employed as an expectorant, antispasmodic and diaphoretic in such organic disturbances as asthma and bronchial catarrh, etc. . . . Professor Youngken makes absolutely no mention of this humble plant as being dangerous or poisonous, although he does state that the taste of the freshly collected roots is acrid and biting. However, a few days after the gathered roots have been allowed to dry, they may be used accordingly, i.e., as a medicinal.

From several listeners I received copies of a letter written by the famous down-easterner Kenneth Roberts of Kennebunkport, Maine. This letter appeared in the *Boston Herald* dated May 10, 1943, and under the title, "Skunk Cabbage can be violently poisonous," read in part: "Years ago, I heard that Skunk Cabbage shoots 3 to 5 inches high made acceptable boiled greens, but didn't get around to trying them until 2 years ago, when I brought our cook a handful of fresh-picked shoots, and asked her to boil them like spinach for dinner. When they were brought to the table, I found that two small forkfuls of the green were enough for me because of their bitterness. Mrs. Roberts ate less than half of that. A third member of my family decided not to try them. An hour later, Mrs. Roberts became violently nauseated. By the time I could get a doctor, I had also become extremely ill. Mrs. Robert, after heroic treatment, recovered in four hours. In my own case the spasms of indescribably violent nausea lasted over six hours in spite of morphine injections. The doctor, an able graduate of McGill University, told me later that he was almost certain I wouldn't recover, and that he had several times given me up."

Mr. Roberts continues: "For some months I had been corresponding with Dr. Irvine H. Page of the Lilly Laboratories at Indianapolis relative to experiments. I wrote him a detailed report of it. The Lilly Laboratories at once asked me to ship them 25 pounds of Skunk Cabbage shoots for Dr. Page's use. I did this, and Dr. Page experimented with them. In the following year, the laboratories had me send them a larger amount of the shoots, and Dr. Page continued his experiments. At their end, he wrote me that he had never been able to bring his experiments to a successful conclusion since all the animals on which he experimented invariably died before an effective dose could be studied. In other words, Dr. Page found, just as I had, that Skunk Cabbage shoots can be violently poisonous."

I then wrote both to author Roberts and to the Dr. Page he mentioned in the above letter, and asked, among other matters, *who* had identified the Skunk Cabbage as such, and was not the specimen of the plant in question Green Hellebore, which grows in the vicinity of Skunk Cabbage?

And these are the answers that I received from Dr. Page and Mr. Roberts: Dr. Page wrote: "Mr. Roberts was the one who sent me the so-called Skunk Cabbage. I took his word that it was such. Our experiments are concerned merely with making extracts of various sorts and testing them on animals for their ability to lower blood pressure and toxicity. Whether the so-called Skunk Cabbage is Hellebore, I have no notion, but I am sure Mr. Roberts could send you some of the material similar to that which he sent me." And Mr. Roberts wrote me: "What I ate was Hellebore. There is practically no Skunk Cabbage in this section, and almost everyone thinks that Hellebore is Skunk Cabbage. . . . I've had a lot of letters from people whose relatives and acquaintances have been poisoned by what they call Skunk Cabbage, but evidently they'd all eaten Hellebore. Professor Milton Hopkins of the University of Oklahoma, who has quite a reputation as a Skunk Cabbage expert, wrote me. 'Perhaps you really did get pure Skunk Cabbage leaves without any Hellebore mixed in with them, in which case one boiling was completely insufficient to dissolve the raphides, and the resulting illness may, of course, have been due to this fact. I have never eaten the leaves without several par-boilings.' "

SOLOMON'S SEAL—*Polygonatum Officinale* (L.)

Synonym: Sealwort.
Habitat: Rich, shaded woods.
Part Used: The early shoots and roots.
Collection: Spring.

The tender young shoots are of excellent service when prepared (steamed) and served like Asparagus. The roots, however, have long been a source of food throughout the world. In northern Europe, the entire plant, collected in Spring, has been used as a pot herb, and in Turkey and Greece, the poorer people, who no doubt are more healthy than their more fortunate compatriots, eat the early roots (Spring) which they boil with other foods or meats. The Indians of New England and southeastern Canada employed all parts of the herb as food extenders, drying much of the Spring-collected shoots for future use, an art which they taught the English and French colonists.

FALSE SOLOMON'S SEAL—*Smilacina Racemosa*

Habitat: Rich, shaded woods and sides of brooks.
Part Used: Young shoots. Fruits (berries).
Collection: The shoots in Spring, the fruits in mid-Summer.

Although this herb is found side by side with the True Solomon's Seal, two ways to best identify the former is by the cluster of greenish-white flowers first terminating the stem, later to be replaced by the round Summer fruits, which when immature are white, then turning to their characteristic red flecked with purple. (The fruits of the other are blue.)

The early shoots may be eaten as an Asparagus substitute, while the berries may be taken fresh with other fruits or preserved with honey, taken in tablespoonful doses as a food remedy for costiveness.

SPRING BEAUTY—*Claytonia Virginiana*

Habitat: Rich woods.
Part Used: The tuberous roots.

We may make extensive food use of this plant as did the Indians and the early settlers, and like them, we may collect the 1-inch tubers in the Spring. Their taste has been described as crisp and pleasant, suggesting Chestnuts.

This starchy food is best prepared roasted until warm, and eaten as is or added to a soup or stew during the last few minutes of preparation.

The flowers of this plentiful herb appear in April and the seeds ripen in June. It is my suggestion that the seeds be planted in the vegetable garden, there to produce a vast supply of the nutritious herb, with far less toil and trouble than is required with Potatoes or other root vegetables.

WILD STRAWBERRY—*Fragaria Virginiana*

Habitat: In dry soil, open fields.
Part Used: Leaves. Fruits.
Collection: The leaves in August; the ripe fruits are gathered in the morning.

The herbalist has long considered a warm tea of the dried leaves a valuable tonic for convalescents, and with Sweet Fern for children having bowel weakness, with St. Johnswort for bedwetting. And too, the leaves are not irritating to the nervous system as are tea and coffee, and so are used with Mint and Lemon peel as a caffeinless tea substitute. Moreover they do help further alkalize the system.

Many were (and still are) the medicinal properties attributed to the ripened fruits: Herbalist John Gerard claimed that eaten whole they "quench thirst and take away, if they be often used, the rednesse and heate of the body." He was not alone in claiming that a decoction of the leaves and fruits "strengthneth the gummes and fastneth the teeth." Dr. William Meyrick wrote that the fruits "dissolve the tartareous incrustations on the teeth." It has been reported to me that the fruits are used as a dentifrice by: 1. Rubbing the fresh fruit over the teeth; 2. Allowing the juice to remain at least 3 or 4 minutes; and 3. Rinsing with tepid water in which has been dissolved a pinch each of salt and sodium bicarbonate.

The virtues of the fruits are further extolled, being recommended for such people who eat too much and for bleared men who have obscured vision due to a watery discharge. And Herbalist Bancke further claimed "it [the fruit] is good to destroy the web in a man's eyes."

The Indians called it the "heart" berry from its shape and color. They made preserves of them and dried them for winter use. They also used the roots to make a tea for stomach complaints, especially for babies and young children.

The genus *Fragaria* is derived from the Latin *frago* meaning "to emit a sweet odor or fragrance." How well corroborated by Maude G. Peterson's apt remarks that the fruits do not depend only upon their color "as a means of allurement, but send forth upon the breezes a

deliciously perfumed notice that they are ready for
guests. Have you not encountered it and, following its
lead, shared with the robins, bluebirds and downy wood-
peckers the delicious feast? The wild flavor of the berries is beyond the power of cultivation to produce or
retain."

Strawberry Jam

Bruise very fine some scarlet Strawberries, gathered
when quite ripe, and put to them a little juice of red
Currants. Beat and sift their weight in sugar, strew it
over them and put them into a preserving-pan. Slowly
boil 20 minutes, skim and put them in glasses.—*An old
recipe*

Strawberry Water Ice

One large bottle (2 quarts) of scarlet Strawberries,
the juice of Lemon, a pound of sugar and half pint of
water. Mix, first rubbing the fruit through a sieve, and
freeze (chill).

SUMAC—1. *Rhus Glabra.* 2. *Rhus Typhina*

Synonym: 1. Lemonade Tree, Sleek, Smooth Sumac. 2.
    Staghorn-Sumac, Vinegar Tree.
Habitat: Dry soil, roadsides.
Part Used: Flowerheads, early to mid-Summer; the
    fruits as they begin to turn a faint red. Dry much
    of these parts for future use.

To prepare a tasty Summer beverage, steep a heaping teaspoonful of the ground flowers and/or fruits,
fresh or dried, in a cup of hot water. Cover 5 or 6
minutes with a saucer. Stir and strain.

The Indians of upper North America gathered
great quantities of the early berries to make a pleasant
beverage much like lemonade. The tart fruits were
sweetened with Maple syrup, soaked in water until re-

quired for use. The dried Sumac berries were also cooked in water with Maple syrup to yield a hot drink, instead of a cooling one as used in the Summer and Fall, the resultant infusion being employed for its medicinal benefits.

Remember, in preparing an herb tea of either Sumac, use less of the Staghorn than of the Smooth, for the fruits and flowers of the former are far more acid or "sour," the better to remember the synonym, Vinegar Tree.

The fruits of the Staghorn Sumac are distinguished from those of the Smooth variety by their being far more hairy.

SUNFLOWER—*Helianthus Annuus* (L.))

Synonym: Marigold of Peru.
Habitat: Rich soil.
Part Used: Seeds.
Collection: Autumn when the flower head begins to shrivel.

I'm quite sure that many of you know of the Sunflower as the official state flower of Kansas, but did you know that the Sunflower may and should find a valuable place in your every-day diet, and as an effective medicinal remedy? Some years ago at the experimental grounds of the University of Illinois, according to a news report, about 100 acres of Sunflower were planted on good, black Corn and Soybean land as an experimental crop. Experiments performed upon the harvested seeds showed that it was possible to grow Sunflowers as profitably as Soybeans. The scientists processed the seeds, which yielded an olive-like oil and buckwheat-like flour, and not only did the oil and flour retain their natural freshness for an extraordinary length of time, they also yielded a high percentage in protein and oil content.

Dr. H. H. Mitchell, University of Illinois protein

expert, has asserted that Sunflower seeds contain 53% protein, which is much higher than any of the present corn-belt crops; moreover—and this is the important factor— their protein is highly digestible and should be included in the human diet and animal feeding.

This news report had me soon looking through my notes on Sunflower and I came across this clipping taken from a most informative magazine, *Organic Gardening* — which all should read whether gardeners or not. "After reading Mr. Rodale's booklet on 'Sunflower Seed — The Miracle Food' and having had severe eye trouble for many years, I decided to try the seeds. I ate a good sized handful each day and in about two weeks noticed a definite and almost unbelievable change. The strain, ache and pain almost completely disappeared, and I could work the entire day and not be conscious of any trouble. I also noticed my hair became more oily where before it had been dry and brittle. Sunflower seeds have been a Godsend, and I heartily recommend them to all who have similar ailments."

Not only was Sunflower a staple food of the North American Indian tribes, but, too, it was known in prehistoric times, because quantities of seeds of the cultivated Sunflower have been found in the remains of dwellings of a people which lived in caves in the Ozark Mountains long before any known historic tribes.

Whenever I think of Sunflower and its relationship with any of the Indian tribes, I am usually reminded of an ancient custom associated with a regional variety of Sunflower called Balsam Root—the root of which is the only part used as a food. This particular custom, or ritual, deals with the Thompson Indians of British Columbia. The past generations have cooked and eaten the roots of this particular variety; moreover, they used to regard it as a mysterious thing, and observed a number of taboos in connection with it; for example, women who engaged in digging or cooking the root must practice extreme cleanliness, and no man might come near the oven where the women ate the first berries, roots or other products of the season. They addressed a prayer to the Sunflower as follows: "I inform thee that I intend to eat thee. Mayest thou always help me to ascend, so that I may always be able to reach the tops of mountains, and I may never be clumsy. I ask this from thee, Sunflower root. Thou art the greatest of all in mystery." To omit this prayer would make the eater lazy and cause him to sleep long in the morning.

The Indians of Eastern Canada used the oil from Sunflower seeds to anoint their hair. The Teton-Dakota prepared a remedy for pulmonary affections by boiling the Sunflower heads from which the bracts were first removed. The Zuni used the roots (with two other herbs) to cure rattlesnake bite. The wound was first sucked by the theurgist who, when satisfied he had extracted as much poison as possible, chewed bits of the three roots and applied the mass to the wound with a bandage. The treatment was repeated each day until the morning of the fifth day, when an Indian woman of the same fraternity as the theurgist washed the patient's head with Yucca suds while the theurgist prayed for his recovery.

And a bit more of geography: Agronomists and naturalists agree that Sunflower makes an excellent soil improver since the growing herb is extremely useful for drying damp soils because of its remarkable ability to absorb quantities of water. Swampy sections in Holland have been made habitable by the extensive cultivation of the Sunflower, and as a result the malarial miasma (marsh miasmata) is absorbed and nullified while abundant oxygen is emitted.

Sunflower was much reverenced by the Aztecs of Mexico and Peru. The early Spanish conquerors found in the Aztec temples numerous representations of the

Sunflower wrought in pure gold. In these temples of the Sun, the priestesses were crowned with Sunflower and carried them in their hands.

Why is it called Sunflower? If you will note that its Latin name is *Helianthus annus*, you will soon discover that, first of all, *Helianthus* is derived from two Greek words, *Helios*, the sun, and *Anthus*, flower. *Annuus* merely means that the Sunflower is an annual plant.

You will realize to your amazement that every part of this plant may be utilized for some important, economic purpose. To be sure, we all know about the seeds; but did you know that even the leaves, the stems and the flowers have been also employed in many useful ways? So, too, have the pith (the interior of the stalk) and the entire plant itself.

The leaves have been included in cattle and poultry food, while the fibres of the stems have long been successfully used by the Chinese in the manufacture of paper and they have admixed the fibres with their silks.

Even the sun-ray flowers offer their services in the form of a color-fast yellow dye—a fact which Mrs. Thomas Healy, the dye expert of our Herb Class, now has ascertained despite her very modest "Why, I never knew that before" smile of hers. She will continue her experiments to obtain a variety with onion skins and Sunflower petals of yellow to orange dyes.

Did you know that the pith of the stalk, i.e. the soft inside of the stem or stalk, is one of the lightest substances known? Since it is ¼ as light as Elder pith or Cork, it has been employed especially in the manufacture of life-saving equipment.

And, finally, after the already mentioned components have been removed from the plant and used to some economic advantage, the remaining refuse, so to speak, is ground up and applied as an organic fertilizer directly as a mulch to the rows of vegetables. Such refuse may be also incorporated in the inevitable compost piles, of which there should be at least one in every corner of your vegetable garden plot. By so saving such a valuable soil-fortifier, you may be assured of a very cheap but plentiful supply of potash. At no time do I recommend the burning of any organic or vegetable waste, as tree leaves and twigs, or Corn or Sunflower stalks, but since the Sunflower stalks are such a most reliable source of potash, they have been burned in small heaps to obtain the residual ash—and of this ash 62% is composed of potash.

Now, during the winter months, we may not be so much concerned with gardens and fertilizers unless we're indulging in that good old winter pastime of arm-chair gardening via the seed catalogues. We do, however, want to know at this time, of what use are these Sunflower seeds? Oh, sure, some of you may say, "I remember way back when Grandma used to roast them on the old cook-stove and we would nibble all afternoon while we did our house chores." But do you recall that several old-timers, cronies of Grandfather, fed their chickens *unroasted* Sunflower seeds and proved to themselves then, as one authority today claims, that fowl that were fed on bruised Sunflower seeds far surpassed in laying power other chickens or fowl not on a Sunflower diet. These seeds, therefore, will offer to the poultry raiser an ever-present source of rich chicken food. (And that's not chicken feed, either!)

What is more to the point is that we humans may also benefit by this "miracle food." The seeds, as I've already said, contain about 50% oil resembling Olive Oil in many respects, for which it may often be substituted to good advantage. The oil is used also in manufacture of a variety of soaps and candles. It is claimed, too, that as a drying oil, it is equal to linseed oil and is unrivalled as a lubricant.

SUNFLOWER - SEED FLOUR: Composition compared with that of other flours and flour supplements.[1]

Food	Moisture	Food energy per 100 grams cal.	% Crude Protein	% Fat	% Carbohydrate	% Calcium	% Phosphorus	Vitamin A value	Thiamine mg.	Riboflavin mg.	Niacin mg.
								Vitamins per 100 grams			
Sunflower-seed flour	4.6	362	52.8	4.5	27.5[2]	.57	58	[3]	3.6	.48	30.0
Cornmeal, white, degerminated	12	355	7.5	1.1	78.8	.01	.14	0	.16	.09	.9
Rye flour, light	11	358	8.9	.9	78.5	.02	.28	0	.15	.07	.9
Soy flour	9	283	42.5	6.5	13.6	.24	.61	110	.82	.34	2.6
Wheat flour, patent	12	355	10.8	.9	75.9	.02	.09	0	.07	.03	.8
Wheat flour, patent, enriched	12	355	10.8	.9	75.9	.02	.09	0	.44	.26	3.5
Wheat flour, whole	11	360	13.0	2.0	72.4	.04	.38	0	.56	.12	5.6
Milk, dried defatted[4]	3.5	359	35.6	1.0	52.0	1.03	1.03	40	.35	1.96	1.1

1. In this table the terms sunflower-seed *flour* and sunflower-seed *meal* are used to describe the same product: *meal* is used when speaking of its use in livestock feeding: *flour* when speaking of its human use. Except for sunflower-seed flour, the analyses given in this table are taken from Miscellaneous Publication No. 572 of the U.S. Department of Agriculture issued in 1945.

2. Not including crude fiber.

3. There are, however, 4.2 milligrams of Carotene (Pro-vitamin A) per pound of meal.

4. Dry skim milk.

After the oil has been expressed from the seeds, the residue today is *not* discarded as waste as in years gone by, but constitutes a practical and much-desired food for cattle and offers its plus benefits also to sheep, pigs, rabbits and poultry. Want a good substitute for coffee? A most enjoyable drink may be had by roasting ripe seed-shells.

Now a brief mention of the food values of the seeds of this herb in question. The facts are: These seeds contain 50-55% protein to the Soybean's 40%, and about 35% of natural fats, which is twice that of Soybean. A recent report of the experimental laboratories of the University of Illinois states that the protein of Sunflower seeds is nearly 100% digestible and therefore is also almost completely assimilable by the body. Moreover, a bulletin issued by the Department of Agriculture of the University of Indiana stated that Sunflower seeds are a rich source of the Vitamin B group, superior to Wheat or Corn germ or defatted Soybean meal.

As a meat substitute, it should be noted, says Alfred W. McCann in *The Science of Eating*, "The Sunflower seeds, either meal or crushed, contain far more protein than meats, eggs, or cheese, and much mineral content because of its deeply penetrating roots. Sunflower seeds are not only free from putrefactive bacteria which abound in meats; the meal of the seeds may be prepared as meat substitutes."

TANSY—*Tanacetum Vulgare*

Synonym: Bitter Buttons, Yellow Buttons.
Part Used: Leaves collected in Spring up to 2nd week
    of May. Leaves and flowering tops (Summer).
Habitat: Waste places.

Said Gerard, "In the Spring time are made with the leaves hereof newly sproong up, and with egs cakes or tansies which be pleasant in taste, and good for the stomacke; for if bad humours cleave thereunder, it doth perfectly concoct them and carry them off." Use the Spring-collected leaves.

This balsamic plant can be used as a substitute for nutmeg and cinnamon.

John Evelyn (*Acetaria*): "Tansy: hot and cleansing but in regard to its domineering Relish, sparingly mixed with our cold Sallet, and much fitter (tho' in very small quantity) for the Pan, being qualify'd with the juices of other fresh Herbs, Spinach, Green Corn, Violet, Primrose-leaves, etc., at entrance of the Spring, and then fry'd brownish, is eaten hot, with the juice of Orange and sugar, as one of the most agreeable of all the boil'd Herbaceous Dishes."

Samuel Pepys, diarist: "Made a pretty dinner for some guests, to wit: 'A brace of stewed carps, six roasted chickens and a jowl of salmon, hot, for the first course; a Tansy and two neat's tongues, and cheese, the second."

Herbalist William Coles had suggested that Springtime requires Tansy's valued seasoning for most foods, that Tansy is "very wholesome" to counteract the saltiness of the large quantities of fish consumed during Lent and the general ill-effects which "the moist and cold constitution of winter has made on people."

Mrs. Stella B. Forrest (Fitchburg, Mass.), Secretary of the Fitchburg Herb Club, includes bits of the young leaves in her puddings to give extra flavor and color; and also in her cottage cheese.

Centuries ago, herb Tansy was rubbed onto and sprinkled over meats to preserve and protect them from flies and ants.

Its chief use is as a culinary herb, an excellent substitute for Sage, with which to flavorize one's foods— fish, meats and, as stated above, cookies, cakes and puddings.

SOW THISTLE—*Sonchus* Species

Habitat: Waste places, in humus-filled soil.
Part Used: Tender leaves, prepared like Wild Lettuce.
Collection: Spring.

We have found a plentiful supply of the *Sonchus* seedlings in mounds of leaf composting piles, in the company of Burdock, Wild (prickly) Lettuce and Hollyhocks, which now serve us well as food, later as medicinal remedies.

Sow Thistle is not recommended as a green or salad herb even though friend John Parkinson did say in 1640 that the leaves "are usually eaten as salat herbes in the Spring. . . . by those beyond the seas familiarly." However, they should be steamed and seasoned with culinary herbs, oil and Lemon juice, or used in soups as suggested for other pot herbs.

TREFOIL—*Oxalis Acetosella* (L.)

Synonym: Shamrock, Wood Sorrel.
Habitat: Waste places. Shade of walls, foundation of
    homes.
Part Used: Upper half.
Collection: Whenever available.

Trefoil may be substituted for any of the Sorrel or Cress species and adds its distinctive tartness to a cole slaw or Summer salad. Always eat it uncooked with soured cream, Swiss or cottage cheese.

This delicate little plant grows in the most shaded parts of our back yards usually along fences and the foundations of homes. It is called Trefoil, "three leaves," since each of its thin leaves is divided into three heart-shaped leaflets. I imagine that this particular leaf structure must have been well noted by the Indian Medicine Man, who would recommend to a brave suffering with a heart ailment either to eat the leaves raw, as in a salad, or else drink a tea brewed with Trefoil. Today, while this is no "sure cure," the practice is the same, the general idea being that this herb directs its benefits to the kidneys and blood, therefore indirectly to the heart. It requires no deep imagination to realize that the thrifty folk of Ireland and other lands knew well of this herb and of its being tasty and most nourishing to one well or ailing.

The 17th of March, as many of you know, is celebrated as St. Patrick's day by the people of Irish descent. On that day you will see many wearing green carnations or other flowers symbolizing the significance of that particular holiday. "The green carnation or other flower" so mentioned is actually considered to simulate or represent the Shamrock of Ireland, which has long been presumed to be (though incorrectly) our own three-leaved Red Clover plant. The Red Clover is *not* the true Shamrock of Ireland.

VIOLET—*Viola* Species

Synonym: Wild Okra.
Habitat: Gardens, roadsides.
Part Used: Leaves and flowers.
Collection: Spring.

The flowers and leaves are even today, as they were in the 1700's, employed by many for their emollient and expectorant properties in bronchitis. The Spring-collected leaves and flowers should be eaten by all as a possible preventive and corrective of bronchial disorders. It is therefore especially recommended for those asthmatic and catarrh-sinus conditions.

The leaves are also eaten in salad (preferably), steamed with Lemon peel, and the young leaves, being rather mucilaginous, are used by some to thicken soups and stews, and for this reason one variety is called Wild Okra.

"The floures are good for inflammations especially of the sides and lungs," wrote Dr. Gerard in his *Herball* (1597). "They take away the hoarseness of the chest, the ruggedness of the wind-pipe and jawes, and take away thirst. There is likewise made of Violets and sugar certaine plates called Sugar Violet, Violet tables or Plate; which is most pleasant and wholesome, especially it comforteth the heart and the other inward parts."

WALNUT—*Juglans Cinerea*

The White Walnut brings back happy childhood days when our herbalist grandfather and the three Harris children went "exploring" for Oilnuts or Butternuts as they are more popularly known. When we got hungry, we would roast the nuts in a quickly improvised open-air fire. A plentiful supply was soon obtained and we were sure that no meal during the next two weeks would be without the Butters. Moreover we saved the green hulls, which were used to prepare "colors," and grandfather was sure to reward us by dyeing the girls' doll dresses tan or light brown and my favorite bows and arrows a dark brown.

When the nuts ripen in late Fall, the still sticky greenish brown husks are best left alone in an attic where they will separate from the nuts. Thus, there is no need of staining the fingers by pounding open the fresh husks. The nut meats will be found to be tender and pleasantly highly-flavored, the better to eat them as closely to the natural state as possible.

Writing in the *American Botanist*, one correspondent declared that the hulling of Walnuts, as usually performed, "is a dirty and disagreeable task, for the juice stains the hands a deep brown very hard to get off. There is, however, a cleaner and easier way of removing the hulls to which Mr. W.W. Ashe has called the editor's attention. It is simply to bore a hole slightly larger in diameter than a hulled Walnut through a piece of maple or other hard wood, and then drive the Walnut through it. This not only removes the hulls, but does it quicker than any other way with which we are acquainted."

The nut-meats may be added to soups just before serving; or cooked with stews or meats already suggested, with other nuts. Contents: Calcium, Magnesium, Phosphorus, Potassium, and Sulphur. Fat—56%. Protein 28%. Walnuts are best eaten with acid fruits and green vegetables.

To pickle White Walnuts, said Henry Hartshorne in his *Household Cyclopedia*, "Pare green Walnuts very thin till the white appears, then throw them into spring water with a handful of salt; keep them under water 6 hours, simmer but do not boil them 5 minutes; remove and put them in cold water and salt; they must be kept quite under the water with a board, otherwise they will not pickle white; dry carefully with cloth and put them into the jar, with some blades of Mace and Nutmeg cut thin. Mix the spice between the nuts and pour vinegar over them; when the jar is full of nuts, pour mutton fat over them and tie them close down to keep out the air."

Syruped Walnuts

Soak a few in cold water for a week, stirring them morning and night. Then boil them until soft, allow to drain and remove the green skin with a coarse cloth. Cook them until soft in a thin syrup of brown sugar, to which is previously added a small stick of Cinnamon and a few Cloves.

WATERCRESS—*Nasturtium Officinale*
"Eat Cress and Learn More Wit"
Habitat: Gravelly, gently moving brooks.

Part Used: The leaves.

Collection: In the late Spring to early Summer. Do not gather if the bottom of the brook is muddy. Three or four cuttings may be taken during the growing season.

This herb is a close relative of our common garden Nasturtium, and is found growing abundantly in many of our native brooks. It has long been relished by the old-timers who knew that no plate of salad vegetables was ever to be without friend Watercress. The tender young shoots have long been used as a salad green in soups and stews and as a decorative garnish, but are not recommended unless eaten with the foods so garnished.

Since ancient times, says Professor Medsger, Watercress has been known as a food. "Xenophon highly recommended it to the Persians and in Western India this was prized by the Mohammedans. The Romans considered it as the food for those who had deranged minds. Lord Bacon urged the people of England to use it."

Even in New England many people have bought this tasty green in markets at a fancy high price but it is to be doubted that the average person (or the Watercress purchaser) can recognize it growing in the trout brook right in back of his own home.

Though the Spartans of old knew naught of the Vitamins of B Complex, they were quick to evaluate the efficacy of this herb's priceless ingredients. They would eat much Watercress with their bread, and soon "became noted for their wit and decision of character."

Several years ago, while conducting a field trip with the members of the Museum Herb Class, I came across two swarthy looking men who were gathering several basketsful of Watercress. The surprise came not because we had something in common, i.e. utilizing common herbs for food value—but because of what one of the

Cress pickers said: "Most Americans don't know how to live because they don't know what is good for them to eat. For as long as I remember, Watercress has always been included in each and every one of our meals. And," he added, pointing to the other whom I had mistakenly called his brother, "this is my father." (The father's youthful appearance, I later discovered, was due to eating such native greens as Watercress and Dandelion and native nuts instead of meats.)

Watercress is an outstanding example of nature's vast sources of food. It is an excellent source of Vitamin C plus A, B, E, and G. Its high Vitamin C content makes it an admirable food for the elderly since the Vitamin C, especially of Watercress, will help to better maintain the suppleness of small blood vessels and thus help to ward off hardening of the arteries.

Dr. Karl Mason of Vanderbilt University had shown that the *dried* leaves of Watercress contained three times as much Vitamin C as the leaves of Lettuce. Moreover, Watercress may well boast of its content of such health-fortifying minerals as sodium, potassium, and calcium, plus those that are constantly required to strengthen the blood stream, namely sulphur, iron and copper and manganese.

Whenever possible include Watercress in a summer salad. *Always eat uncooked.* And as Dr. Meyrick puts it: "It is undoubtedly an excellent antiscorbutic and stomachic (tonic) and there is no better way of using it than as a salad." The herb is most succulent and most perishable and therefore should be kept moist and in the refrigerator.

There are many recipes which call for Watercress, but these cannot be recommended simply because the finished products are most unhygienic and contain very little of the herb's nutritional benefits. Examples of such recipes: Watercress and Potato Soup, Chicken Watercress Pie, and Watercress Pinwheel Biscuits. However, when serving an omelette or soup, sprinkle a tablespoonful of the finely minced leaves over the foods just before serving.

Note: For further information regarding the cultivation and propagation of Watercress, see J. H. Beattie, *Production of Watercress*, United States Dept. of Agriculture, 1938.

Composition of Fresh Watercress (1 pound)			*Composition of Spinach* (3 qts.)
Protein	7.7	Gm	8.6
Fat	1.4	Gm	1.1
Carbohydrate	15.0	Gm	11.9
Calcium	885	Mg	301
Phosphorus	209	Mg	205
Iron	9.1	Mg	11.2
Vitamin A	21,450	I.U.	35,040
Thiamine (Vitamin B_1)	.37	Mg	.41
Riboflavin	.71	Mg	.76
Niacin	3.6	Mg	2.2
Vitamin C (Ascorbic Acid)	350	Mg	219

WINTERCRESS—*Barbarea Vulgaris*

Synonym: Yellow Rocket.

Habitat: Wet, rich soils.

Part Used: The leaves.

Collection: Spring, Fall, and even up to December, on St. Barbara's day, the generic name thus emphasizing its out-of-season availability. Gather the leaves until the plant's flowers show their full yellow.

The herb has been unjustly abandoned, only because it is not recognized as a plentiful source of excellent greens. And when it does grow in profusion in one's garden it is relegated to the "rubbish-weed pile," there to join the other unknowns that have been discarded as worthless. Indeed!

Treat the early leaves and new stems with kindness. Please do not boil the leaf too long in hot water, for then its value as an efficacious antiscorbutic will be lost. If your taste of Wintercress does not allow the glossy green leaves as a fresh salad ingredient, then steaming them but a few minutes in a very little hot water is permissible. Season with Garlic, vinegar and oil.

WINTERGREEN—*Gaultheria Procumbens* (L.)

Synonym: Checkerberry, Mountain Tea, Teaberry, Partridgeberry.
Habitat: Sandy, rocky areas beneath evergreen trees.
Part Used: Leaves. Fruits (berries).
Collection: The leaves, Spring to early Summer; the berries, later Summer to Spring.

The young leaves are oval, shining and with a reddish tinge, and their aromatic flavor makes for a most palatable and refreshing substitute for Pekoe tea. Thus the synonyms, Teaberry and Mountain Tea. To prepare the infusion, a teaspoonful of the dried finely ground leaves is stirred well in a cupful of hot water and covered 5 minutes; then stirred and strained. Such a tea must be sipped slowly.

However, the globular red fruits possess a like spicy flavoring and like the leaves may be used in preparation of a tisane or to add flavor to Pekoe tea, or they may be added even to soups.

Bibliography

Bailey, L. H. — *Standard Cyclopedia of Horticulture*, 3 vols., Macmillan Co., N. Y.

Barrett, S. A. — *Material Aspects of Pomo Culture*, Public Museum of Milwaukee, 1952.

Blair, E. H. — *Indian Tribes of Upper Mississippi and Great Lakes Region*, Cleveland, 1911.

Blanchan, Neltje — *Nature's Garden*, New York, 1900.

Britton, Nathaniel Lord, and Brown, Addison — *Illustrated Flora of the Northern United States and Canada*, 2nd ed., New York, 1913.

Burr, Fearing — *Field and Garden Vegetables of America*, Boston, 1865.

Candolle, Alphonse de — *Origin of Cultivated Plants*, New York, 1885.

Carter, George F. — "Some Hopi Indian Foods," *The Herbarist*, Boston, 1946.

Dana, Mrs. William Starr — *How to Know the Wild Flowers*, Charles Scribners Sons, New York, 1898.

Emerson, George B. — *A Report on the Trees and Shrubs Growing Naturally in the Forests of Massachusetts*, 2nd ed., Boston, 1875.

Esser, William L. — *Dictionary of Foods*, John's Island, S. C., 1947.

Fogg John Milton — *Weeds of Lawn and Garden*, Philadelphia, 1945.

Georgia, Ada E. — *A Manual of Weeds*, New York, 1925.

Gerard, John — *The Herball, or Generall Historie of Plantes*, London, 1597.

Gilmore, Melvin R. — *Indian Lore and Indian Gardens*, Ithaca, N.Y., 1930.

Green, Thomas — *Universal Herbal*, 2 vols., London, 1823.

Harris, Ben Charles — *Better Health with Culinary Herbs*, Boston, 1952; *Kitchen Medicines*, Barre, 1968.

Hartshorne, Henry — *Household Cyclopedia*, Philadelphia, 1871.

Healthful Living Digest — Winnepeg, Manitoba, Canada.

Henderson, W. A. — *Modern Domestic Cookery*, New York.

Holt, Rackham — *George Washington Carver*, Doubleday and Co., New York, 1943.

Kalm, Peter — *Travels of North America*, 2nd ed., London, 1772.

Keeler, Harriet L. — *Our Northern Shrubs*, New York, 1903.

Le Maout, Emmanuel, and Decaisne, J. — *A General System of Botany*, translated from the original by Mrs. Hooker, with additions, an appendix and synopsis by J. D. Hooker, London, 1873.

Lindley, John — *Flora Medica*, London, 1838.

Lounsberry, Alice — *A Guide to the Trees*, New York, 1900.

Medsger, Oliver Perry — *Edible Wild Plants*, Macmillan Co., New York, 1939.

Meyer, Joseph E. — *The Herbalist*, Indiana Botanic Gardens, 1934.

Meyrick, William — *New Family Herbal*, London, 1740.

Mooney, James, and Olbrechts, Frank M. — *The Swimmer Manuscript*, Smithsonian Institution, Bureau of American Ethnology, Bulletin 99, Washington, D.C., 1932.

Muenscher, Walter C. — *Weeds*, New York, 1935.

New England Farmer — Vols. 1850-62, Boston.

Palmer, Edward — *Food Products of the North American Indians*, U.S. Department of Agriculture, Annual Report, 1870.

Parkinson, John, *Theatrum Botanicum, the Theater of Plantes*, London, 1640.

Peterson, Maude Gridley — *How to Know Wild Fruits*, New York, 1905.

Pfeiffer, Ehrenfried — *The Earth's Face and Human Destiny*, Rodale Press, Emmaus, Pa., 1947.

Ray, W. W. — *Common Edible Mushrooms of Oklahoma*, Vol. 40, No.10, Oklahoma Agricultural and Mechanical College, Stillwater, 1943.

Robbins, Wilfred W., and Ramaley, Francis — *Plants Useful to Man*, Philadelphia, 1933.

Rohde, Eleanor Sinclair — *A Garden of Herbs*, Boston, 1936.

Rogers, Julia E. — *The Tree Book*, Doubleday, Page, and Co., New York, 1905.

Saunders, Charles F. — *Useful Wild Plants of the United States and Canada*, Robert M. McBride, New York, 1920.

Smith, Huron H. — *Ethnobotany of the Ojibwe Indians*, Bulletin of the Public Museum of the City of Milwaukee, 1932; *Ethnobotany of the Forest Potawatomi Indians*, Bulletin of the Public Museum of the City of Milwaukee, 1933.

Smithsonian Institution — 44th Annual Report of the Bureau of American Ethnology, Washington, D.C., 1926-1927.

Stratton, Robert — *Edible Wild Greens and Salads of Oklahoma*, Oklahoma Agricultural and Mechanical College, Stillwater, Okla.

Sturtevant, Edward Lewis — *Notes on Edible Plants*, edited by U. P. Hedrick, J. B. Lyon Co., Albany, N. Y., 1919.

Youngken, Heber W. — *Textbook of Pharmacognosy*, Philadelphia, 1936.

Index